Zero Hour
and other modern stories

Zero Hour

and other modern stories

edited by Michael Swan

Cambridge University Press

Cambridge

London   New York   New Rochelle

Melbourne   Sydney

Published by the Press Syndicate of the University of Cambridge
The Pitt Building, Trumpington Street, Cambridge CB2 IRP
32 East 57th Street, New York, NY 10022, U.S.A.
296 Beaconsfield Parade, Middle Park, Melbourne 3206,
Australia

Selection, notes and questions © Cambridge University Press 1977

ISBN 0 521 21545 5

First published 1977
Reprinted 1980

Reproduced, printed and bound in Great Britain by
Cox & Wyman Ltd, Reading

Contents

Preface

The stories in this book have been specially selected for advanced students of English. They have not been altered in any way, but can be read easily without a dictionary.

Some difficult words are marked like this*: they are explained in the glossary that comes immediately after each story. (Note that these brief explanations are intended only to help you *understand* the meaning of the words as they are used in the text; if you want to use the words yourself in other situations, you will need to get more complete information from a teacher or a good dictionary.) Some difficult words are not explained because their meaning can easily be guessed, or because they are not important for an understanding of the story.

After the story there are some questions and topics for discussion; the questions will help you to see how well you have understood the story, and the discussion topics will give you a chance to say what you think about it.

M.S.

Acknowledgements

The editor and publishers are grateful to the following for permission to reproduce these stories:
Maurice Shadbolt and Curtis Brown Ltd. for the use of 'The People Before', which first appeared in *Summer Fires and Winter Country* (1963); John Wain and Curtis Brown Ltd. for the use of 'A Message from The Pig-Man' from *Nuncle and Other Stories* (1960); Muriel Spark and Harold Ober Associates Inc. (NY) for 'You Should Have Seen the Mess' from *The Go-Away Bird and Other Stories* (1958); Alan Paton and Jonathan Cape Ltd. for the use of 'Ha'-penny', which first appeared in *Debbie Go Home*; Ray Bradbury and A. D. Peters & Co. for the use of 'Zero Hour' from *The Illustrated Man*; The Estate of Joyce Cary and Curtis Brown Ltd. for the use of 'The Breakout' from *Spring Song and Other Stories*. 'The Little Girl and the Wolf', 'The Shrike and the Chipmunks', 'The Rabbits Who Caused all the Trouble' and 'The Unicorn in the Garden' from *Vintage Thurber* by James Thurber © 1963 Hamish Hamilton.

Alan Paton
Ha'penny*

*Alan Paton (born in 1903) is a South African writer who
works for the improvement of race relations and social conditions
in his country. His best-known novel,* Cry the Beloved
Country, *was published in 1948; it made him famous, and
at the same time attracted worldwide attention to the racial
problem in South Africa. 'Ha'penny' is a short and simple, but
very moving story about a homeless boy who has been sent to a
school for young lawbreakers. It may be partly autobiographical:
Paton was himself the principal of a boys' reformatory for
some years.*

Of the six hundred boys at the reformatory,* about one
hundred were from ten to fourteen years of age. My
Department had from time to time expressed the inten-
tion of taking them away, and of establishing a special
institution for them, more like an industrial school than
a reformatory. This would have been a good thing, for
their offences were very trivial,* and they would have
been better by themselves. Had such a school been established, I should have liked to be Principal of it myself,
for it would have been an easier job; small boys turn
instinctively towards affection, and one controls them by
it, naturally and easily.

Some of them, if I came near them, either on parade*
or in school or at football, would observe me watchfully,

not directly or fully, but obliquely* and secretly; sometimes I would surprise them at it, and make some small sign of recognition, which would satisfy them so that they would cease to observe me, and would give their full attention to the event of the moment. But I knew that my authority was thus confirmed and strengthened.

The secret relations with them were a source of continuous pleasure to me. Had they been my own children I would no doubt have given a greater expression to it. But often I would move through the silent and orderly parade, and stand by one of them. He would look straight in front of him with a little frown of concentration that expressed both childish awareness* and manly indifference to my nearness. Sometimes I would tweak* his ear, and he would give me a brief smile of acknowledgement, or frown with still greater concentration. It was natural, I suppose, to confine these outward expressions to the very smallest, but they were taken as symbolic, and some older boys would observe them and take themselves to be included. It was a relief, when the reformatory was passing through times of turbulence* and trouble, and when there was danger of estrangement* between authority and boys, to make those simple and natural gestures, which were reassurances to both me and them that nothing important had changed.

On Sunday afternoons when I was on duty I would take my car to the reformatory and watch the free boys being signed out at the gate. This simple operation was watched by many boys not free, who would tell each other, 'In so many weeks I'll be signed out myself.' Among the watchers were always some of the small boys, and these I would take by turns in the car. We would go out to the Potchefstroom Road with its ceaseless stream of traffic, and to the Baragwanath crossroads, and come back by the Van Wyksrus road to the reformatory. I would talk to them about their families, their parents, their sisters and brothers, and I would pretend to know nothing of Durban, Port Elizabeth, Potchefstroom, and Clocolan, and ask them if these places were bigger than Johannesburg.

One of the small boys was Ha'penny, and he was about twelve years old. He came from Bloemfontein and was the biggest talker of them all. His mother worked in a white person's house, and he had two brothers and two sisters. His brothers were Richard and Dickie, and his sisters Anna and Mina.

'Richard and Dickie?' I asked.

'Yes, meneer.'*

'In English,' I said, 'Richard and Dickie are the same name.'

When we returned to the reformatory, I sent for Ha'-penny's papers; there it was plainly set down, Ha'penny was a waif,* with no relatives at all. He had been taken in from one home to another, but he was naughty and uncontrollable, and eventually had taken to* pilfering* at the market.

I then sent for the Letter Book, and found that Ha'-penny wrote regularly, or rather that others wrote for him till he could write himself, to Mrs Betty Maarman, of 48 Vlak Street, Bloemfontein. But Mrs Maarman had never once replied to him. When questioned, he had said, perhaps she is sick. I sat down and wrote at once to the Social Welfare Officer at Bloemfontein, asking him to investigate.

The next time I had Ha'penny out in the car I questioned him again about his family. And he told me the same as before, his mother, Richard and Dickie, Anna

3

and Mina. But he softened the 'D' of Dickie, so that it
sounded now like Tickie.

'I thought you said Dickie,' I said.

'I said Tickie,' he said.

He watched me with concealed* apprehension,* and
I came to the conclusion that this waif of Bloemfontein
was a clever boy, who had told me a story that was all
imagination, and had changed one single letter of it to
make it safe from any question. And I thought I understood it all too, that he was ashamed of being without a
family and had invented them all, so that no one might
discover that he was fatherless and motherless and that
no one in the world cared whether he was alive or dead.
This gave me a strong feeling for him, and I went out
of my way* to manifest* towards him that fatherly care
that the State, though not in those words, had enjoined
upon me* by giving me this job.

Then the letter came from the Social Welfare Officer
in Bloemfontein, saying that Mrs Betty Maarman of 48
Vlak Street was a real person, and that she had four
children, Richard and Dickie, Anna and Mina, but that
Ha'penny was no child of hers, and she knew him only
as a derelict* of the streets. She had never answered his
letters, because he wrote to her as 'Mother', and she was
no mother of his, nor did she wish to play any such role.*
She was a decent woman, a faithful member of the
church, and she had no thought of corrupting* her family
by letting them have anything to do with such a child.

But Ha'penny seemed to me anything but* the usual
delinquent,* his desire to have a family was so strong,
and his reformatory record was so blameless, and his
anxiety to please and obey so great, that I began to feel
a great duty towards him. Therefore I asked him about
his 'mother'.

He could not speak enough of her, nor with too high praise. She was loving, honest, and strict. Her home was clean. She had affection for all her children. It was clear that the homeless child, even as he had attached himself to me, would have attached himself to her; he had observed her even as he had observed me, but did not know the secret of how to open her heart, so that she would take him in, and save him from the lonely life that he led.

'Why did you steal when you had such a mother?' I asked.

He could not answer that; not all his brains nor his courage could find an answer to such a question, for he knew that with such a mother he would not have stolen at all.

'The boy's name is Dickie,' I said, 'not Tickie.'

And then he knew the deception* was revealed. Another boy might have said, 'I told you it was Dickie,' but he was too intelligent for that; he knew that if I had established* that the boy's name was Dickie, I must have established other things too. I was shocked by the immediate and visible effect of my action. His whole brave assurance* died within him, and he stood there exposed,* not as a liar, but as a homeless child who had surrounded himself with mother, brothers, and sisters, who did not exist. I had shattered* the very foundations of his pride, and his sense of human significance.*

He fell sick at once, and the doctor said it was tuberculosis. I wrote at once to Mrs Maarman, telling her the whole story, of how this small boy had observed her, and had decided that she was the person he desired for his mother. But she wrote back saying that she could take no responsibility for him. For one thing, Ha'penny was a Mosuto,* and she was a coloured* woman; for another,

5

Alan Paton

she had never had a child in trouble, and how could she take such a boy?

Tuberculosis is a strange thing; sometimes it manifests itself suddenly in the most unlikely host, and swiftly sweeps* to the end. Ha'penny withdrew himself* from the world, from all Principals and mothers, and the doctor said there was little hope. In desperation I sent money for Mrs Maarman to come.

She was a decent, homely woman, and, seeing that the situation was serious, she, without fuss or embarrassment, adopted Ha'penny for her own. The whole reformatory accepted her as his mother. She sat the whole day with him, and talked to him of Richard and Dickie, Anna and Mina, and how they were all waiting for him to come home. She poured out her affection on him, and had no fear of his sickness, or did she allow it to prevent her from satisfying his hunger to be owned. She talked to him of what they would do when he came back, and how he would go to the school, and what they would buy for Guy Fawkes* night.

He in his turn gave his whole attention to her, and when I visited him he was grateful, but I had passed out of his world. I felt judged in that I had sensed only the existence and not the measure* of his desire. I wished I had done something sooner, more wise, more prodigal.*

We buried him on the reformatory farm, and Mrs Maarman said to me, 'When you put up the cross, put he was my son.'

'I'm ashamed,' she said, 'that I wouldn't take him.'

'The sickness,' I said, 'the sickness would have come.'

'No,' she said, shaking her head with certainty. 'It wouldn't have come. And if it had come at home, it would have been different.'

So she left for Bloemfontein, after her strange visit to

6

a reformatory. And I was left too, with the resolve to be more prodigal in the task that the State, though not in so many words, had enjoined upon me.

Glossary

page 1
Ha'penny : halfpenny
reformatory : school for young lawbreakers
trivial : unimportant
on parade : lined up (like soldiers) to be inspected

page 2
obliquely : sideways
awareness : consciousness
tweak : pull suddenly
turbulence : disturbance
estrangement : bad relations

page 3
meneer : Afrikaans word for sir
waif : homeless child
had taken to : had started
pilfering : stealing small things

page 4
concealed : hidden
apprehension : fear
I went out of my way : I made a special effort
manifest : show
enjoined upon me : given me as my responsibility
derelict : person abandoned by everybody
play any such role : have any such position
corrupting : damaging the morals of
anything but : anything except
delinquent : lawbreaker

page 5
deception : lie
established : found out
assurance : confidence
exposed : revealed
shattered : broken to pieces
significance : meaning, importance
Mosuto : member of an African tribe
coloured : word used in South Africa for people of mixed race

page 6
sweeps : goes very quickly
withdrew himself : took himself away
Guy Fawkes night : on November 5th, 1605, Guy Fawkes was
   arrested while trying to blow up Parliament with gun-
   powder. The event is still celebrated with bonfires and
   fireworks on November 5th each year
measure : quantity, strength
prodigal : generous

Questions

1 The narrator (the person who tells the story) says that the
   younger boys would have been better by themselves (page
   1 line 8). Why do you think this is?
2 Why did Ha'penny write to Mrs Maarman?
3 Why did he want people to believe that she was his
   mother?
4 Why didn't she want to accept him?
5 Why did he change the name 'Dickie' to 'Tickie'?
6 Why did the narrator take a special interest in Ha'penny?
7 The narrator says 'I thought I understood it all, too'
   (page 4 line 9). What didn't he understand?
8 What was the effect on Ha'penny of having his lies found
   out?

Topics for discussion

1 What do you think of the narrator's treatment of Ha'penny? Would you have behaved differently towards him? If so, how?

2 Do you think the narrator was responsible for Ha'penny's death?

3 What do you think his purpose was when he asked 'Why did you steal when you had such a mother' (page 5 line 10)?

4 Do you think Mrs Maarman was right to reject Ha'penny?

5 Do you think this kind of reformatory is the best way of dealing with young criminals?

6 Do you think that unhappiness or emotional insecurity can cause illness and even death?

7 Do you like the story? Why (not)?

Muriel Spark
You Should Have Seen the Mess*

Muriel Spark was born in 1918, and grew up in Edinburgh. She first became well known as a writer with the publication of her novel The Comforters *in 1957; other novels include* The Prime of Miss Jean Brodie *(which has been filmed), and* The Ballad of Peckham Rye. *She has also published poetry and a number of short stories. 'You Should Have Seen the Mess' is about a young working-class girl: it is written in the first person, as if the girl herself were telling the story. She is obsessed with cleanness, and this causes problems for her in her relationships with other people. One of the most interesting features of the story is the extremely skilful way in which the girl's character is shown through her actions, her thoughts, and above all the kind of language she uses.*

I am now more than glad that I did not pass into the grammar school* five years ago, although it was a disappointment at the time. I was always good at English, but not so good at the other subjects!!

I am glad that I went to the secondary modern school,* because it was only constructed the year before. Therefore, it was much more hygienic* than the grammar school. The secondary modern was light and airy, and the walls were painted with a bright, washable gloss.* One day, I was sent over to the grammar school, with a note for one of the teachers, and you should have seen the mess! The corridors were dusty, and I saw dust on the window ledges,* which were chipped.* I saw into one of the classrooms. It was very untidy in there.

I am also glad that I did not go to the grammar school, because of what it does to one's habits. This may appear to be a strange remark, at first sight. It is a good thing to have an education behind you, and I do not believe in ignorance, but I have had certain experiences, with educated people, since going out into the world.

I am seventeen years of age, and left school two years ago last month. I had my A certificate for typing, so got my first job, as a junior, in a solicitor's* office. Mum was pleased at this, and Dad said it was a first-class start, as it was an old-established firm. I must say that when I went for the interview, I was surprised at the windows, and the stairs up to the offices were also far from clean. There was a little waiting-room, where some of the elements were missing from the gas fire, and the carpet on the floor was worn. However, Mr Heygate's office, into which I was shown for the interview, was better. The furniture was old, but it was polished, and there was a good carpet, I will say that. The glass of the bookcase was very clean.

I was to start on the Monday, so along I went. They took me to the general office, where there were two senior shorthand-typists, and a clerk, Mr Gresham, who was far from smart in appearance. You should have seen the mess!! There was no floor covering whatsoever,* and so dusty everywhere. There were shelves all round the room with old box files on them. The box files* were falling to pieces, and all the old papers inside them were crumpled.* The worst shock of all was the tea-cups. It was my duty to make tea, mornings and afternoons. Miss Bewlay showed me where everything was kept. It was kept in an

old orange box, and the cups were all cracked. There
were not enough saucers to go round, etc. I will not go
into* the facilities,* but they were also far from hygienic.
After three days, I told Mum, and she was upset, most
of all about the cracked cups. We never keep a cracked
cup, but throw it out, because those cracks can harbour*
germs.* So mum gave me my own cup to take to the
office.

Then at the end of the week, when I got my salary,
Mr Heygate said, 'Well, Lorna, what are you going to
do with your first pay?' I did not like him saying this, and
I nearly passed a comment, but I said, 'I don't know.'
He said, 'What do you do in the evenings, Lorna? Do
you watch Telly?' I did take this as an insult, because we
call it T.V. and his remark made me out to be unedu-
cated. I just stood, and did not answer, and he looked
surprised. Next day, Saturday, I told Mum and Dad
about the facilities, and we decided I should not go back
to that job. Also, the desks in the general office were
rickety.* Dad was indignant, because Mr Heygate's concern* was flourishing,* and he had letters after his name.

Everyone admires our flat, because Mum keeps it
spotless, and Dad keeps doing things to it. He has done
it up all over, and got permission from the Council* to
remodernize the kitchen. I well recall the Health Visitor,*
remarking to Mum, 'You could eat off your floor, Mrs
Merrifield.' It is true that you could eat your lunch off
Mum's floors, and any hour of the day or night you will
find every corner spick and span.*

Next, I was sent by the agency* to a publisher's for an
interview, because of being good at English. One look
was enough!! My next interview was a success, and I am
still at Low's Chemical Co. It is a modern block, with a
quarter of an hour rest period, morning and afternoon.

Mr Marwood is very smart in appearance. He is well spoken, although he has not got a university education behind him. There is special lighting over the desks, and the typewriters are the latest models.

So I am happy at Low's. But I have met other people, of an educated type, in the past year, and it has opened my eyes. It so happened that I had to go to the doctor's house, to fetch a prescription* for my young brother, Trevor, when the epidemic* was on. I rang the bell, and Mrs Darby came to the door. She was small, with fair hair, but too long, and a green maternity dress.* But she was very nice to me. I had to wait in their living-room, and you should have seen the state it was in! There were broken toys on the carpet, and the ash trays were full up. There were contemporary* pictures on the walls, but the furniture was not contemporary, but old-fashioned, with covers which were past standing up to another wash,* I should say. To cut a long story short, Dr Darby and Mrs Darby have always been very kind to me, and they meant everything for the best. Dr Darby is also short and fair, and they have three children, a girl and a boy, and now a baby boy.

When I went that day for the prescription, Dr Darby said to me, 'You look pale, Lorna. It's the London atmosphere. Come on a picnic* with us, in the car, on Saturday.' After that I went with the Darbys more and more. I liked them, but I did not like the mess, and it was a surprise. But I also kept in with them for the opportunity of meeting people, and Mum and Dad were pleased that I had made nice friends. So I did not say anything about the cracked lino,* and the paintwork all chipped. The children's clothes were very shabby for a doctor, and she changed them out of their school clothes when they came home from school, into those worn-out garments. Mum always kept us spotless to go out to play, and I do not like to say it, but those Darby children frequently looked like the Leary family, which the Council evicted* from our block,* as they were far from houseproud.

One day, when I was there, Mavis (as I called Mrs Darby by then) put her head out of the window, and shouted to the boy, 'John, stop peeing* over the cabbages at once. Pee on the lawn.' I did not know which way to look. Mum would never say a word like that from the window, and I know for a fact that Trevor would never pass water outside, not even bathing in the sea.

I went there usually at the week-ends, but sometimes on week-days, after supper. They had an idea to make a match* for me with a chemist's assistant, whom they had taken up too. He was an orphan,* and I do not say there was anything wrong with that. But he was not accustomed to those little extras that I was. He was a good-looking boy, I will say that. So I went once to a dance, and twice to films with him. To look at, he was quite clean in appearance. But there was only hot water at the week-end at his place, and he said that a bath once a week was sufficient. Jim (as I called Dr Darby by then) said it was sufficient also, and surprised me. He did not have much money, and I do not hold that against him. But there was no hurry for me, and I could wait for a man in a better position, so that I would not miss those little extras. So he started going out with a girl from the coffee bar, and did not come to the Darbys very much then.

There were plenty of boys at the office, but I will say this for the Darbys, they had lots of friends coming and going, and they had interesting conversation, although sometimes it gave me a surprise, and I did not know where to look. And sometimes they had people who were very down and out,* although there is no need to be. But most of the guests were different, so it made a comparison with the boys at the office, who were not so educated in their conversation.

Now it was near the time for Mavis to have her baby, and I was to come in at the week-end, to keep an eye on the children, while the help had her day off. Mavis did not go away to have her baby, but would have it at home, in their double bed, as they did not have twin beds, although he was a doctor. A girl I knew, in our block, was engaged, but was let down,* and even she had her baby in the labour ward.* I was sure the bedroom was not hygienic for having a baby, but I did not mention it.

One day, after the baby boy came along; they took me in the car to the country, to see Jim's mother. The baby was put in a carry-cot at the back of the car. He began to cry, and without a word of a lie, Jim said to him over his shoulder, 'Oh shut your gob,* you little bastard.'* I did not know what to do, and Mavis was smoking a cigarette. Dad would not dream of saying such a thing to Trevor or I. When we arrived at Jim's mother's place, Jim said, 'It's a fourteenth-century cottage, Lorna.' I could well believe it. It was very cracked and old, and it made one wonder how Jim could let his old mother live in this tumble-down* cottage, as he was so good to everyone else. So Mavis knocked at the door, and the old lady came. There was not much anyone could do to the inside. Mavis said, 'Isn't it charming, Lorna?' If that was a joke, it was going too far. I said to the old Mrs Darby, 'Are you going to be re-housed?' but she did not understand this, and I explained how you have to apply to the Council, and keep at them.* But it was funny that the Council had not done something already, when they go round condemning.* Then old Mrs Darby said, 'My dear, I shall be re-housed in the Grave.' I did not know where to look.

There was a carpet hanging on the wall, which I think was there to hide a damp spot.* She had a good T.V. set, I will say that. But some of the walls were bare brick, and the facilities were outside, through the garden. The furniture was far from new.

One Saturday afternoon, as I happened to go to the Darbys, they were just going off to a film and they took me too. It was the Curzon, and afterwards we went to a flat in Curzon Street. It was a very clean block, I will say that, and there were good carpets at the entrance. The couple there had contemporary furniture, and they also spoke about music. It was a nice place, but there was no Welfare Centre to the flats, where people could go for social intercourse, advice, and guidance. But they were well spoken, and I met Willy Morley, who was an artist. Willy sat beside me, and we had a drink. He was young, dark, with a dark shirt, so one could not see right away if he was clean. Soon after this, Jim said to me, 'Willy wants to paint you, Lorna. But you'd better ask your Mum.' Mum said it was all right if he was a friend of the Darbys.

I can honestly say that Willy's place was the most unhygienic place I have seen in my life. He said I had an unusual type of beauty, which he must capture.* This was when we came back to his place from the restaurant. The light was very dim, but I could see the bed had not been made, and the sheets were far from clean. He said he must paint me, but I told Mavis I did not like to go back there. 'Don't you like Willy?' she asked. I could not deny that I liked Willy, in a way. There was something about him, I will say that. Mavis said, 'I hope he hasn't been making a pass* at you, Lorna.' I said he had not done so, which was almost true, because he did not attempt to go to the full extent.* It was always unhygienic when I went to Willy's place, and I told him so once, but he said, 'Lorna, you are a joy.' He had a nice way, and he took me out in his car, which was a good one, but dirty inside, like his place. Jim said one day, 'He has pots of money, Lorna,' and Mavis said, 'You might make a man of him, as he is keen on you.' They always said Willy came from a good family.

But I saw that one could not do anything with him. He would not change his shirt very often, or get clothes, but he went round like a tramp,* lending people money, as I have seen with my own eyes. His place was in a terrible mess, with the empty bottles, and laundry in the corner. He gave me several gifts over the period, which I took as he would have only given them away, but he never tried to go to the full extent. He never painted my portrait, as he was painting fruit on a table all that time, and they said his pictures were marvellous, and thought Willy and I were getting married.

One night, when I went home, I was upset as usual, after Willy's place. Mum and Dad had gone to bed, and I looked round our kitchen which is done* in primrose and white. Then I went into the living room, where Dad has done one wall in a patterned paper, deep rose and white, and the other walls pale rose, with white woodwork. The suite* is new, and Mum keeps everything beautiful. So it came to me, all of a sudden, what a fool I was, going with Willy. I agree to equality, but as to me marrying Willy, as I said to Mavis, when I recall his place, and the good carpet gone greasy, not to mention the paint oozing out of the tubes, I think it would break my heart to sink so low.

Glossary

page 10
mess: untidiness, dirt
Grammar School: for children over 11 who are more successful at traditional school subjects
Secondary Modern School: for other children
hygienic: clean, with no danger to health
gloss: shiny paint

page 11
window ledges: small shelves under the windows
chipped: the paint was damaged
solicitor: a kind of lawyer
whatsoever: at all
files: holders for keeping papers in order
crumpled: not flat and smooth

page 12
go into: discuss in detail
facilities: she means the lavatory (toilet)
germs: small creatures which can cause illness, microbes
can harbour germs: germs can live there
rickety: not solid, unsteady
concern: business
flourishing: doing very well
Council: local government
Health Visitor: from the health department of the council
spick and span: very clean and tidy
agency: an organization that finds jobs for people

page 13
prescription: paper from a doctor with the name of the medicine you need
epidemic: outbreak of disease among a lot of people
maternity dress: dress worn by a woman who is going to have a baby
contemporary: in a modern style

past standing up to another wash: too old to wash again
picnic: meal in the open air
lino: hard shiny floor-covering

page 14
evicted: made them leave their home
block: block of flats
peeing: pissing (vulgar), passing water (usually
    done in a lavatory)
to make a match: to arrange a marriage
orphan: child with no parents

page 15
down and out: very poor
she was let down: her boyfriend left her when she was
    pregnant
labour ward: room in a hospital where women have their
    babies
gob: a rude word for mouth
bastard: a swearword (rude word) used to insult a person
tumble-down: falling down
keep at them: keep asking them
condemning: saying that old houses must be pulled down

page 16
damp: a bit wet
capture: succeed in putting into a picture
making a pass: trying to kiss her, for example

page 17
to go to the full extent: to have sex with her, make love to her
tramp: somebody poor and badly dressed who has no home
    and lives on the roads
done: decorated
suite: set of furniture

Questions

1 Why was the girl glad that she didn't go to a grammar school?
2 Why did she dislike her first employer asking her 'Do you watch Telly'?
3 Why do you think she didn't go to work for the publisher who interviewed her?
4 What is the girl's attitude to educated people?
5 Why was she embarrassed when Jim's mother said 'I shall be rehoused in the grave'?
6 What did she mean by saying that the chemist's assistant 'was not accustomed to those little extras that I was'?
7 Why was she upset, at the end of the story, when she went home from Willy's place?

Topics for discussion

1 Discuss the character of the girl who tells the story. Do you like her or not? Do you know people like her? What do you think are her greatest problems in life?
2 What is her social background, and what sort of attitudes does she have to social class?
3 What is her attitude to the Darby family, and what problems does this relationship present for her?
4 What is her attitude to Willy, and why does this relationship break down?
5 What different kinds of 'untidiness' does the girl dislike? Do you agree or disagree with her feelings?
6 Discuss the language used by the girl in telling the story. What expressions does she often repeat, and what do these tell us about her character?
7 Look very carefully at the last paragraph but one ('But I

saw ... getting married') and analyse the way in which the sentences are constructed.

8 Do you like the story? If so, why? If not, what kind of writers or subjects do you prefer?

James Thurber

Four Fables for Our Time

James Thurber (1894–1962) was an American writer and artist who worked for the New Yorker *magazine, and published a number of books. He is widely regarded as one of the greatest modern humorists. In his 'Fables of Our Time', he adapts the classical fable form to modern conditions. These short pieces are always amusing, but many of them (such as 'The Rabbits who Caused all the Trouble') also contain a serious commentary on human behaviour.*

The Little Girl and the Wolf

One afternoon a big wolf waited in a dark forest for a little girl to come along carrying a basket of food to her grandmother. Finally a little girl did come along and she was carrying a basket of food. 'Are you carrying that basket to your grandmother?' asked the wolf. The little girl said yes, she was. So the wolf asked her where her grandmother lived and the little girl told him and he disappeared into the wood.

When the little girl opened the door of her grandmother's house she saw that there was somebody in bed with a nightcap and nightgown on. She had approached no nearer than twenty-five feet from the bed when she saw that it was not her grandmother but the wolf, for even in a nightcap a wolf does not look any more like your grandmother than the Metro-Goldwyn lion* looks like Calvin Coolidge.* So the little girl took an automatic* out of her basket and shot the wolf dead.

Moral: It is not so easy to fool little girls nowadays as it used to be.

The Shrike* and the Chipmunks*

Once upon a time there were two chipmunks, a male and a female. The male chipmunk thought that arranging nuts in artistic patterns was more fun than just piling them up to see how many you could pile up. The female was all for piling up as many as you could. She told her husband that if he gave up making designs with the nuts there would be room in their large cave for a great many more and he would soon become the wealthiest chipmunk in the woods. But he would not let her interfere with his designs, so she flew into a rage and left him. 'The shrike will get you,' she said, 'because you are helpless and cannot look after yourself.' To be sure, the female chipmunk had not been gone three nights before the male had to dress for a banquet* and could not find his studs* or shirt or suspenders.* So he couldn't go to the banquet, but that was just as well, because all the chipmunks who did go were attacked and killed by a weasel.*

The next day the shrike began hanging around outside the chipmunk's cave, waiting to catch him. The shrike couldn't get in because the doorway was clogged up* with soiled* laundry and dirty dishes. 'He will come out for a walk after breakfast and I will get him then,' thought the shrike. But the chipmunk slept all day and did not get up and have breakfast until after dark. Then he came out for a breath of air before beginning work on a new design. The shrike swooped down to snatch up the chipmunk, but could not see very well on account of the dark, so he batted his head against an alder* branch and was killed.

A few days later the female chipmunk returned and saw the awful mess the house was in. She went to the bed and shook her husband. 'What would you do without me?' she demanded. 'Just go on living, I guess,' he said. 'You wouldn't last five days,' she told him. She swept the house and did the dishes and sent out the laundry, and then she made the chipmunk get up and wash and dress. 'You can't be healthy if you lie in bed all day and never get any exercise,' she told him. So she took him for a walk in the bright sunlight and they were both caught and killed by the shrike's brother, a shrike named Stoop.

*Moral: Early to rise and early to bed makes a male healthy and wealthy and dead.**

The Rabbits who Caused all the Trouble

Within the memory of the youngest child there was a family of rabbits who lived near a pack of wolves. The wolves announced that they did not like the way the rabbits were living. (The wolves were crazy about* the way they themselves were living, because it was the only way to live.) One night several wolves were killed in an earthquake* and this was blamed on the rabbits, for it is well known that rabbits pound on the ground* with their hind* legs and cause earthquakes. On another night one of the wolves was killed by a bolt of lightning and this was also blamed on the rabbits, for it is well known that lettuce-eaters cause lightning. The wolves threatened to civilize the rabbits if they didn't behave,* and the rabbits decided to run away to a desert island. But the other animals, who lived at a great distance, shamed them,* saying, 'You must stay where you are and be brave. This is no world for escapists. If the wolves attack you, we will come to your aid, in all probability.' So the rabbits continued to live near the wolves and one day there was a terrible flood which drowned a great many wolves. This was blamed on the rabbits, for it is well known that carrot-nibblers* with long ears cause floods. The wolves descended on the rabbits, for their own good, and imprisoned them in a dark cave, for their own protection.

When nothing was heard about the rabbits for some weeks, the other animals demanded to know what had happened to them. The wolves replied that the rabbits had been eaten and since they had been eaten the affair was a purely internal matter. But the other animals warned that they might possibly unite against the wolves unless some reason was given for the destruction of the rabbits. So the wolves gave them one. 'They were trying to escape,' said the wolves, 'and, as you know, this is no world for escapists.'

Moral : Run, don't walk, to the nearest desert island.

The Unicorn* in the Garden

Once upon a sunny morning a man who sat in a breakfast nook* looked up from his scrambled eggs to see a white unicorn with a gold horn quietly cropping* the roses in the garden. The man went up to the bedroom where his wife was still asleep and woke her. 'There's a unicorn in the garden,' he said. 'Eating roses.' She opened one unfriendly eye and looked at him. 'The unicorn is a mythical beast,'* she said, and turned her back on him. The man walked slowly downstairs and out into the garden. The unicorn was still there; he was now browsing* among the tulips. 'Here unicorn,' said the man, and he pulled up a lily and gave it to him. The unicorn ate it gravely. With a high heart, because there was a unicorn in his garden, the man went upstairs and roused his wife again. 'The unicorn,' he said, 'ate a lily.' His wife sat up in bed and looked at him, coldly. 'You are a booby,'* she said, 'and I am going to have you put in the booby-hatch.'* The man, who had never liked the words 'booby' and 'booby-hatch', and who liked them even less on a shining morning when there was a unicorn in the garden, thought for a moment. 'We'll see about that,' he said. He walked over to the door. 'He has a golden horn in the middle of his forehead,' he told her. Then he went back to the garden to watch the unicorn; but the unicorn had gone away. The man sat down among the roses and went to sleep.

As soon as the husband had gone out of the house, the wife got up and dressed as fast as she could. She was very excited and there was a gloat* in her eye. She telephoned the police and she telephoned a psychiatrist; she told them to hurry to her house and bring a strait-jacket.* When the police and the psychiatrist arrived they sat down in chairs and looked at her, with great interest. 'My husband,' she said, 'saw a unicorn this morning.' The police looked at the psychiatrist and the psychiatrist looked at the police. 'He told me it ate a lily,' she said. The psychiatrist looked at the police and the police looked at the psychiatrist. 'He told me it had a golden horn in the middle of its forehead,' she said. At a solemn signal from the psychiatrist, the police leaped from their chairs and seized the wife. They had a hard time subduing her,* for she put up a terrific struggle, but they finally

subdued her. Just as they got her into the strait-jacket, the husband came back into the house.

'Did you tell your wife you saw a unicorn?' asked the police. 'Of course not,' said the husband. 'The unicorn is a mythical beast.' 'That's all I wanted to know,' said the psychiatrist. 'Take her away. I'm sorry, sir, but your wife is as crazy as a jay bird.' So they took her away, cursing and screaming, and shut her up in an institution. The husband lived happily ever after.

*Moral: Don't count your boobies until they are hatched.**

Glossary

The Little Girl and the Wolf
page 23
The Metro-Goldwyn lion: symbol of the Metro-Goldwyn-Mayer film company
Calvin Coolidge: president of the U.S.A. 1923–8
automatic: automatic pistol

The Shrike and the Chipmunks
page 24
shrike: kind of bird
chipmunks: small animals like squirrels found in North America
banquet: important dinner
studs: things for fixing detachable collars onto shirts
suspenders: straps that go over the shoulders and hold up trousers
weasel: a fierce small animal
clogged up: blocked
soiled: dirty
alder: kind of tree

page 25
early to rise . . . : there is a traditional saying 'Early to bed and early to rise makes a man healthy and wealthy and wise'.

The Rabbits who Caused all the Trouble
page 26
were crazy about : loved
earthquake : movement of the earth
pound on the ground : hit the ground
hind : back
behave : obey the rules, be good
shamed them : made them ashamed of their wish to run away
to nibble : to eat (with small bites)

The Unicorn in the Garden
page 28
unicorn : imaginary animal in old stories with one horn in the
    middle of its forehead
nook : little corner
cropping : eating
mythical beast : animal that doesn't exist
browsing : eating
booby : mad person (slang)
booby-hatch : mental hospital (slang)
gloat : expression of triumph
strait-jacket : special jacket for controlling mad people when
    they are violent

page 29
subduing her : getting her under control

page 30
don't count . . . : there is an expression 'Don't count your
    chickens until they are hatched' (= until they are out of the
    eggs)

Questions

1 *The Little Girl and the Wolf* is a variation on a traditional
    children's story (called 'Little Red Riding Hood' in
    English). Do you know how the original story ends?

2   Who do you think the male and female chipmunk represent?

3   Who do you think the rabbits, the wolves, and the other animals represent?

4   Explain the double meaning in the expression 'a purely internal matter'. Can you find any other ironical or satirical expressions in the story about the rabbits?

5   How is the ending of 'The Unicorn in the Garden' different from what we (and the woman) expect? Can you explain in your own words what the moral means?

Topics for discussion

1   Which of these stories do you like best? Why?

2   Do you find them funny? Why (not)?

3   What picture does Thurber seem to have of marriage? Do you know any married couples who behave like the two chipmunks? Which one of them do you sympathize with?

4   Can you think of any real political situation which (in your opinion) is similar to that in 'The Rabbits who Caused all the Trouble?'

John Wain
A Message from the Pig-Man

This story is about a small boy, Eric, whose father has left home. Eric is trying to understand the disturbing world he lives in: there are a large number of things that puzzle him, and one of the most frightening is the mysterious 'Pig-man'. Although the story is told in the third person, there is a deliberately childish quality in the descriptions and use of language, which makes it appear as if Eric himself is talking. John Wain, the author, started as a university teacher of English, but gave this up to become a professional writer; he has published novels, short stories, poetry and criticism.

He was never called Ekky now, because he was getting to be a real boy, nearly six, with grey flannel* trousers that had a separate belt, and weren't kept up by elastic, and his name was Eric. But this was just one of those changes brought about naturally, by time, not a disturbing alteration; he understood that. His mother hadn't meant that kind of change when she had promised, 'Nothing will be changed.' It was all going to go on as before, except that Dad wouldn't be there, and Donald would be there instead. He knew Donald, of course, and felt all right about his being in the house, though it seemed, when he lay in bed and thought about it, mad and pointless* that Donald's coming should mean that Dad had to go. Why should it mean that? The house was quite big. He hadn't any brothers and sisters, and if he *had* had any he wouldn't have minded sharing his bedroom, even with a baby that wanted a lot of looking after, so long as it left the spare room free for Dad to sleep in. If he did that, they wouldn't have a spare room, it was true, but then, the spare room was nearly always empty; the last time anybody had used the spare room was *years* ago, when he had been much smaller – last winter, in fact. And, even then, the visitor, the lady with the funny teeth who laughed as she breathed in, instead of as she breathed out like everyone else, had only stayed two or three nights. *Why* did grown-ups* do everything in such a mad, silly way? They often told him not to be silly, but they were silly themselves in a useless way, not laughing or singing or anything, just being silly and sad.

It was so hard to read the signs; that was another thing. When they did give you something to go on, it was impossible to know how to take it. Dad had bought him a train, just a few weeks ago, and taught him how to fit the lines together. That ought to have meant that he would stay; what sensible person would buy a train, and fit it all up ready to run, even as a present for another person – *and then leave*? Donald had been quite good about the train, Eric had to admit that; he had bought a bridge for it and a lot of rolling-stock.* At first he had got the wrong kind of rolling-stock, with wheels too close together to fit on to the rails; but instead of playing the usual grown-ups' trick of pulling a face* and then not doing anything about it, he had gone back to the shop, straight away that same afternoon, and got the right kind. Perhaps that meant *he* was going to leave. But that didn't seem likely. Not the way Mum held on to him all the time, even holding him round the middle as if he needed keeping in one piece.

All the same, he was not Ekky now, he was Eric, and he was sensible and grown-up. Probably it was his own fault that everything seemed strange. He was not living up to* his grey flannel trousers – perhaps that was it; being afraid of too many things, not asking questions that would probably turn out to have quite simple answers.

The Pig-man, for instance. He had let the Pig-man worry him far too much. None of the grown-ups acted as if the Pig-man was anything to be afraid of. He probably just *looked* funny, that was all. If, instead of avoiding him so carefully, he went outside one evening and looked at him, took a good long, unafraid look, leaving the back door open behind him so that he could dart* in to the safety and warmth of the house . . . no! It was better, after all, not to see the Pig-man; not till he was bigger, anyway; nearly six was quite big but it wasn't really *very* big. . . .

And yet it was one of those puzzling things. No one ever told him to be careful not to let the Pig-man get hold of him, or warned him in any way; so the Pig-man *must* be harmless, because when it came to anything that *could* hurt you, like the traffic on the main road, people were always ramming it into you* that you must look both ways, and all that stuff. And yet when it came to the Pig-man, no one ever mentioned him; he seemed beneath the notice of grown-ups. His mother would say, now and then, 'Let me see, it's today the Pig-man comes, isn't it?' or, 'Oh dear, the Pig-man will be coming round soon, and I haven't put anything out.' If she talked like this, Eric's spine* would tingle* and go cold; he would keep very still and wait, because quite often her next words would be, 'Eric, just take these peelings,'* or whatever it was, 'out to the bucket, dear, will you?' The

35

bucket was about fifty yards away from the back door; it was shared by the people in the two next-door houses. None of *them* was afraid of the Pig-man, either. What was their attitude, he wondered? Were they sorry for him, having to eat damp old stuff out of a bucket – tea-leaves and eggshells and that sort of thing? Perhaps he cooked it when he got home, and made it a bit nicer. Certainly, it didn't look too nice when you lifted the lid of the bucket and saw it all lying there. It sometimes smelt, too. Was the Pig-man very poor? Was he sorry for him-self, or did he feel all right about being like that? *Like what?* What did the Pig-man look like? He would have little eyes, and a snout* with a flat end; but would he have trotters,* or hands and feet like a person's?

Lying on his back, Eric worked soberly* at the prob-lem. The Pig-man's bucket had a handle; so he must carry it in the ordinary way, in his hand – unless, of course, he walked on all fours and carried it in his mouth. But that wasn't very likely, because if he walked on all fours, what difference would there be between him and an ordinary pig? To be called the Pig-man, rather than the Man-pig, surely implied that he was up-right, and dressed. Could he talk? Probably, in a kind of grunting* way, or else how would he tell the people what kind of food he wanted them to put in his bucket? *Why hadn't he asked Dad about the Pig-man?* That had been his mistake; Dad would have told him exactly all about it. But he had gone. Eric fell asleep, and in his sleep he saw Dad and the Pig-man going in a train together; he called, but they did not hear him and the train carried them away. 'Dad!' he shouted desperately after it. 'Don't bring the Pig-man when you come back! Don't bring the Pig-man!' Then his mother was in the room, kissing him and smelling nice; she felt soft, and the softness ducked* him into sleep, this time without dreams; but the next day his questions returned.

Still, there was school in the morning, and going down to the swings* in the afternoon, and altogether a lot of different things to crowd out the figure of the Pig-man and the questions connected with it. And he was never further from worrying about it all than that moment, a few evenings later, when it suddenly came to a crisis.

Eric had been allowed, 'just for once', to bring his train into the dining-room after tea, because there was a fire there that made it nicer than the room where he usually played. It was warm and bright, and the carpet in front of the fireplace was smooth and firm, exactly right for laying out the rails on. Donald had come home and was sitting – in Dad's chair, but never mind – reading the paper and smoking. Mum was in the kitchen, clattering* gently about, and both doors were open so that she and Donald could call out remarks to each other. Only a short passage lay between. It was just the part of the day Eric liked best, and bed-time was comfortably far off. He fitted the sections of rail together, glancing in anticipation* at the engine as it stood proudly waiting to haul* the carriages round and round, tremendously fast.

Then his mother called, 'Eric! Do be a sweet, good boy, and take this stuff out to the Pig-man. My hands are covered with cake mixture. I'll let you scrape out* the basin* when you come in.'

For a moment he kept quite still, hoping he hadn't really heard her say it, that it was just a voice inside his head. But Donald looked over at him and said, 'Go along, old man. You don't mind, do you?'

Eric said, 'But tonight's when the Pig-man *comes*.'

Surely, *surely* they weren't asking him to go out, in the

37

deep twilight,* just at the time when there was the greatest danger of actually *meeting* the Pig-man.

'All the better,' said Donald, turning back to his paper.

Why was it better? Did they *want* him to meet the Pigman?

Slowly, wondering why his feet and legs didn't refuse to move, Eric went through into the kitchen. 'There it is,' his mother said, pointing to a brown-paper carrier* full of potato-peelings and scraps.*

He took it up and opened the back door. If he was quick, and darted along to the bucket *at once*, he would be able to lift the lid, throw the stuff in quickly, and be back in the house in about the time it took to count ten.

One – two – three – four – five – six. He stopped. The bucket wasn't there.

It had gone. Eric peered round, but the light, though faint, was not as faint as *that*. He could see that the bucket had gone. *The Pig-man had already been.*

Seven – eight – nine – ten, his steps were joyous and light. Back in the house, where it was warm and bright and his train was waiting.

'The Pig-man's gone, Mum. The bucket's not there.'

She frowned, hands deep in the pudding-basin. 'Oh, yes, I do believe I heard him. But it was only a moment ago. Yes, it was just before I called you, darling. It must have been that that made me think of it.'

'Yes?' he said politely, putting down the carrier.

'So if you nip along,* dear, you can easily catch him up. And I *do* want that stuff out of the way.'

'Catch him up?' he asked, standing still in the doorway.

'Yes, dear, *catch him up*,' she answered rather sharply (the Efficient Young Mother knows when to be Firm).

'He can't possibly be more than a very short way down the road.'

Before she had finished Eric was outside the door and running. This was a technique he knew. It was the same as getting into icy cold water. If it was the end, if the Pig-man seized him by the hand and dragged him off to his hut,* well, so much the worse. Swinging* the paper carrier in his hand, he ran fast through the dusk.*

The back view of the Pig-man was much as he had expected it to be. A slow, rather lurching* gait,* hunched* shoulders, an old hat crushed down on his head (to hide his ears?) and the pail* in his hand. Plod,* plod, as if he were tired. Perhaps this was just a ruse,* though, probably he could pounce* quickly enough when his wicked little eyes saw a nice tasty little boy or something ... did the Pig-man eat birds? Or cats?

Eric stopped. He opened his mouth to call to the Pig-man, but the first time he tried, nothing came out except a small rasping* squeak. His heart was banging like fireworks* going off.* He could hardly hear anything.

'Mr Pig-man!' he called, and this time the words came out clear and rather high.

The jogging* old figure stopped, turned, and looked at him. Eric could not see properly from where he stood. But he *had* to see. Everything, even his fear, sank and drowned in the raging tide of his curiosity. He moved forward. With each step he saw more clearly. The Pig-man was just an ordinary old man.

'Hello, sonny. Got some stuff there for the old grunters?'

Eric nodded, mutely,* and held out his offering. What old grunters? What did he mean?

The Pig-man put down his bucket. He had ordinary hands, ordinary arms. He took the lid off. Eric held out

39

the paper carrier, and the Pig-man's hand actually touched his own for a second. A flood of gratitude rose up inside him. The Pig-man tipped the scraps into the bucket and handed the carrier back.

'Thanks, sonny,' he said.

'Who's it for?' Eric asked, with another rush of articulateness.* His voice seemed to have a life of its own.

The Pig-man straightened up, puzzled. Then he laughed, in a gurgling* sort of way, but not like a pig at all.

'Arh Aarh Harh Harh,' the Pig-man went. 'Not for me, if that's watcher* mean, arh harh.'

He put the lid back on the bucket. 'It's for the old grunters,' he said. 'The old porkers. Just what they likes. Only not fruit skins. I leave a note, sometimes, about what not to put in. Never fruit skins. It gives 'em the belly-ache.'*

He was called the Pig-man because he had some pigs that he looked after.

'Thank you,' said Eric. 'Good-night.' He ran back towards the house, hearing the Pig-man, the ordinary old man, the ordinary usual normal old man, say in his just ordinary old man's voice, 'Good-night, sonny.'

So that was how you did it. You just went straight ahead, not worrying about this or that. Like getting into cold water. You just *did* it.

He slowed down as he got to the gate. For instance, if there was a question that you wanted to know the answer to, and you had always just felt you couldn't ask, the thing to do was to ask it. Just straight out, like going up to the Pig-man. Difficult things, troubles, questions, you just treated them like the Pig-man.

So that was it!

The warm light shone through the crack of the door.

He opened it and went in. His mother was standing at the table, her hands still working the cake mixture about. She would let him scrape out the basin, and the spoon – he would ask for the spoon, too. But not straight away. There was a more important thing first.

He put the paper carrier down and went up to her. 'Mum,' he said. 'Why can't Dad be with us even if Donald *is* here? I mean, why can't he live with us as well as Donald?'

His mother turned and went to the sink. She put the tap on and held her hands under it.

'Darling,' she called.

'Yes?' came Donald's voice.

'D'you know what he's just said?'

'What?'

'He's just asked . . .' She turned the tap off and dried her hands, not looking at Eric. 'He wants to know why we can't have Jack to live with us.'

There was a silence, then Donald said, quietly, so that his voice only just reached Eric's ears, 'That's a hard one.'

'You can scrape out the basin,' his mother said to Eric. She lifted him up and kissed him. Then she rubbed her cheek along his, leaving a wet smear.* 'Poor little Ekky,' she said in a funny voice.

She put him down and he began to scrape out the pudding-basin, certain at least of one thing, that grown-ups were mad and silly and he hated them all, all, *all*.

Glossary

page 33
flannel : a cloth made from wool
pointless : senseless, useless

page 34
grown-ups: a children's word for adults
rolling-stock: the carriages and trucks on a railway
pulling a face: putting on a dissatisfied or unpleasant expression

page 35
living up to his flannel trousers: behaving like a big, sensible boy
   who had the right to wear flannel trousers
dart: run very quickly
ramming it into you: repeating it very often
spine: backbone
tingle: feel as if a small electric current was going through it
peelings: potato peel

page 36
snout: a pig's nose
trotters: a pig's feet
soberly: seriously
grunting: making the noise of a pig

page 37
ducked him: pushed him down
swing: seat hanging on chains for children to play on
clattering: making a noise with plates, saucepans, etc
anticipation: looking forward to something
haul: pull
basin: bowl
scrape out the basin: get out the little bits of pudding that are
   left in the basin

page 38
twilight: the evening half-light
carrier (bag): paper shopping bag
scraps: bits of left-over food
nip: go quickly

page 39
hut: small wooden house
swinging: moving backwards and forwards

dusk: the same as twilight
lurching: moving irregularly from side to side
gait: way of walking
hunched shoulders: shoulders held very high.
pail: bucket
to plod: to walk slowly and heavily
ruse: trick
pounce: jump to attack
rasping: rough
fireworks: explosives (used for celebrations) which produce
   coloured lights and/or loud noises
going off: exploding
jogging: walking or running with short steps
mutely: silently

page 40
articulate: able to talk easily
gurgling: like the noise of water running out of a bath
whatcher: what you
belly-ache: stomach-ache, indigestion

page 41
smear: a wet mark

Questions

1 Why wasn't Eric called 'Ekky' any more?
2 What was the relationship between Eric's mother and
   Donald?
3 How did Eric feel about Donald?
4 How did he feel about his father going away?
5 What did he think the Pig-man was? And what was the
   Pig-man, really?
6 What different examples of adult behaviour did Eric find
   puzzling?
7 Why was he so upset at the end of the story?

John Wain

Topics for discussion

1 The writer has tried to take us inside the head of a five-year-old child, and to show us how he thinks and feels. Do you think he has succeeded?

2 Look at the language used to describe Eric's thoughts. Do you think it's the language of an adult or a child?

3 How would you explain to a child in Eric's situation why his father couldn't live with them?

4 Do you know any families in a similar situation? What is the effect on the children?

5 What do you feel about Eric's mother's behaviour at the end of the story, when she says 'poor little Ekky'?

6 What is the 'message' from the Pig-man?

7 What do you think Eric's worry about the Pig-man really represents?

8 Do you like the story? Why (not)?

H. H. Munro ('Saki')
The Story-Teller

*H. H. Munro (who wrote under the pen-name 'Saki') was
born in 1870 and killed in the First World War. He published
plays and novels, but is best known for his short stories: most of
these are humorous, and they often contain an element of
sadism. Munro was brought up by aunts who treated him
badly, and he never forgot it; in his description of the
children's aunt in this story we can see a certain desire for
revenge.*

It was a hot afternoon, and the railway carriage was cor-
respondingly sultry,* and the next stop was at Templecombe, nearly an hour ahead. The occupants of the
carriage were a small girl, and a smaller girl, and a small
boy. An aunt belonging to the children occupied one
corner seat, and the further corner seat on the opposite
side was occupied by a bachelor who was a stranger to
their party, but the small girls and the small boy emphatically occupied the compartment. Both the aunt
and the children were conversational in a limited, per-
sistent way, reminding one of the attentions of a house-
fly that refused to be discouraged. Most of the aunt's
remarks seemed to begin with 'Don't,' and nearly all of
the children's remarks began with 'Why?' The bachelor
said nothing out loud.

'Don't, Cyril, don't,' exclaimed the aunt, as the small

boy began smacking the cushions of the seat, producing a cloud of dust at each blow.

'Come and look out of the window,' she added.

The child moved reluctantly to the window. 'Why are those sheep being driven out of that field?' he asked.

'I expect they are being driven to another field where there is more grass,' said the aunt weakly.

'But there is lots of grass in that field,' protested the boy; 'there's nothing else but grass there. Aunt, there's lots of grass in that field.'

'Perhaps the grass in the other field is better,' suggested the aunt fatuously.*

'Why is it better?' came the swift, inevitable question.

'Oh, look at those cows!' exclaimed the aunt. Nearly every field along the line had contained cows or bullocks, but she spoke as though she were drawing attention to a rarity.

'Why is the grass in the other field better?' persisted Cyril.

The frown on the bachelor's face was deepening to a scowl.* He was a hard, unsympathetic man, the aunt decided in her mind. She was utterly unable to come to any satisfactory decision about the grass in the other field.

The smaller girl created a diversion by beginning to recite* 'On the Road to Mandalay.'* She only knew the first line, but she put her limited knowledge to the fullest possible use. She repeated the line over and over again in a dreamy but resolute* and very audible* voice; it seemed to the bachelor as though someone had had a bet with her that she could not repeat the line aloud two thousand times without stopping. Whoever it was who had made the wager* was likely to lose his bet.

'Come over here and listen to a story,' said the aunt,

when the bachelor had looked twice at her and once at the communication cord.*

The children moved listlessly* towards the aunt's end of the carriage. Evidently her reputation as a story-teller did not rank high in their estimation.*

In a low, confidential voice, interrupted at frequent intervals by loud, petulant* questions from her listeners, she began an unenterprising* and deplorably* uninteresting story about a little girl who was good, and made friends with everyone on account of her goodness, and was finally saved from a mad bull by a number of rescuers who admired her moral character.

'Wouldn't they have saved her if she hadn't been good?' demanded the bigger of the small girls. It was exactly the question that the bachelor had wanted to ask.

'Well, yes,' admitted the aunt lamely,* 'but I don't think they would have run quite so fast to her help if they had not liked her so much.'

'It's the stupidest story I've ever heard,' said the bigger of the small girls, with immense conviction.

'I didn't listen after the first bit, it was so stupid,' said Cyril.

The smaller girl made no actual comment on the story, but she had long ago recommenced a murmured repetition of her favourite line.

'You don't seem to be a success as a story-teller,' said the bachelor suddenly from his corner.

The aunt bristled* in instant defence at this unexpected attack.

'It's a very difficult thing to tell stories that children can both understand and appreciate,' she said stiffly.

'I don't agree with you,' said the bachelor.

'Perhaps you would like to tell them a story,' was the aunt's retort.

H. H. Munro ('Saki')

'Tell us a story,' demanded the bigger of the small girls.

'Once upon a time,' began the bachelor, 'there was a little girl called Bertha, who was extraordinarily good.'

The children's momentarily-aroused interest began at once to flicker;* all stories seemed dreadfully alike, no matter who told them.

'She did all that she was told, she was always truthful, she kept her clothes clean, ate milk puddings as though they were jam tarts, learned her lessons perfectly, and was polite in her manners.'

'Was she pretty?' asked the bigger of the small girls.

'Not as pretty as any of you,' said the bachelor, 'but she was horribly good.'

There was a wave of reaction in favour of the story; the word horrible in connection with goodness was a novelty* that commended itself.* It seemed to introduce a ring of truth that was absent from the aunt's tales of infant life.

'She was so good,' continued the bachelor, 'that she won several medals for goodness, which she always wore, pinned on to her dress. There was a medal for obedience, another medal for punctuality, and a third for good behaviour. They were large metal medals and they clinked against one another as she walked. No other child in the town where she lived had as many as three medals, so everybody knew that she must be an extra good child.'

'Horribly good,' quoted Cyril.

'Everybody talked about her goodness, and the Prince of the country got to hear about it, and he said that as she was so very good she might be allowed once a week to walk in his park, which was just outside the town. It was a beautiful park, and no children were ever allowed in

48

it, so it was a great honour for Bertha to be allowed to go there.'

'Were there any sheep in the park?' demanded Cyril.

'No,' said the bachelor, 'there were no sheep.'

'Why weren't there any sheep?' came the inevitable question arising out of that answer.

The aunt permitted herself a smile, which might almost have been described as a grin.

'There were no sheep in the park,' said the bachelor, 'because the Prince's mother had once had a dream that her son would either be killed by a sheep or else by a clock falling on him. For that reason the Prince never kept a sheep in his park or a clock in his palace.'

The aunt suppressed a gasp of admiration.

'Was the Prince killed by a sheep or by a clock?' asked Cyril.

'He is still alive, so we can't tell whether the dream will come true,' said the bachelor unconcernedly; 'anyway, there were no sheep in the park, but there were lots of little pigs running all over the place.'

'What colour were they?'

'Black with white faces, white with black spots, black all over, grey with white patches, and some were white all over.'

The story-teller paused to let a full idea of the park's treasures sink into the children's imaginations; then he resumed:

'Bertha was rather sorry to find that there were no flowers in the park. She had promised her aunts, with tears in her eyes, that she would not pick any of the kind Prince's flowers, and she had meant to keep her promise, so of course it made her feel silly to find that there were no flowers to pick.'

'Why weren't there any flowers?'

'Because the pigs had eaten them all,' said the bachelor promptly. 'The gardeners had told the Prince that you couldn't have pigs and flowers, so he decided to have pigs and no flowers.'

There was a murmur of approval at the excellence of the Prince's decision; so many people would have decided the other way.

'There were lots of other delightful things in the park. There were ponds with gold and blue and green fish in them, and trees with beautiful parrots* that said clever things at a moment's notice,* and humming birds that hummed all the popular tunes of the day. Bertha walked up and down and enjoyed herself immensely, and thought to herself: "If I were not so extraordinarily good I should not have been allowed to come into this beautiful park and enjoy all that there is to be seen in it," and her three medals clinked against one another as she walked and helped to remind her how very good she really was. Just then an enormous wolf came prowling* into the park to see if it could catch a fat little pig for its supper.'

'What colour was it?' asked the children, amid an immediate quickening of interest.

'Mud-colour all over, with a black tongue and pale grey eyes that gleamed with unspeakable ferocity.* The first thing that it saw in the park was Bertha; her pinafore* was so spotlessly white and clean that it could be seen from a great distance. Bertha saw the wolf and saw that it was stealing towards her, and she began to wish that she had never been allowed to come into the park. She ran as hard as she could, and the wolf came after her with huge leaps and bounds.* She managed to reach a shrubbery* of myrtle* bushes and she hid herself in one of the thickest of the bushes. The wolf came sniffing among the branches, its black tongue lolling* out of its mouth and its pale grey eyes glaring with rage. Bertha was terribly frightened, and thought to herself: "If I had not been so extraordinarily good I should have been safe in town at this moment." However, the scent of the myrtle was so strong that the wolf could not sniff out where Bertha was hiding, and the bushes were so thick that he might have hunted about in them for a long time without catching sight of her, so he thought he might as well go off and catch a little pig instead. Bertha was trembling very much at having the wolf prowling and sniffing so near her, and as she trembled the medal for obedience clinked against the medals for good conduct and punctuality. The wolf was just moving away when he heard the sound of the medals clinking and stopped to listen; they clinked again in a bush quite near him. He dashed into the bush, his pale grey eyes gleaming with ferocity and triumph and dragged Bertha out and devoured* her to the last morsel.* All that was left of her were her shoes, bits of clothing, and the three medals for goodness.'

'Were any of the little pigs killed?'

'No, they all escaped.'

'The story began badly,' said the smaller of the small girls, 'but it had a beautiful ending.'

'It is the most beautiful story that I ever heard,' said the bigger of the small girls, with immense decision.

'It is the *only* beautiful story I have ever heard,' said Cyril.

A dissentient* opinion came from the aunt.

'A most improper story to tell to young children! You have undermined* the effect of years of careful teaching.'

'At any rate,' said the bachelor, collecting his belongings preparatory to leaving the carriage, 'I kept them quiet for ten minutes, which was more than you were able to do.'

'Unhappy woman!' he observed to himself as he walked down the platform of Templecombe station; 'for the next six months or so those children will assail* her in public with demands for an improper story!'

Glossary

page 45
sultry: hot, with a heavy atmosphere

page 46
fatuously: foolishly
scowl: angry frown
recite: say aloud from memory
'On the road to Mandalay': a poem
resolute: determined
audible: loud and clear
wager: bet

page 47
communication cord: emergency brake
listlessly: without enthusiasm
estimation: opinion
petulant: childishly bad-tempered
unenterprising: unimaginative
deplorably: terribly
lamely: giving an unsatisfactory answer
bristled: reacted angrily

page 48
flicker: sink down, die away
novelty: something new
commended itself: seemed good

page 50
parrots: birds that can imitate speech
at a moment's notice: as soon as you asked them to
prowling: hunting
ferocity: fierceness
pinafore: article of clothing worn over a dress to keep it clean
leaps and bounds: big jumps
shrubbery: group of bushes
myrtle: kind of evergreen bush
lolling: hanging

page 51
devoured: ate
morsel: small piece
dissentient: contradictory
undermined: weakened

page 52
assail: attack

Questions

1 What is meant by 'the small girls and the small boy emphatically occupied the compartment' (page 45 lines 8–9)?
2 Explain the exact meaning of 'the bachelor said nothing out loud' (page 45 line 15).
3 Rewrite in more simple words the sentence 'Evidently her reputation as a story-teller did not rank high in their estimation'.
4 Why didn't the children like the aunt's story?
5 Why did they lose interest in the bachelor's story at the beginning?
6 What different things in the story revived their interest?
7 Why did the aunt smile at the question 'Why weren't there any sheep?' (page 45 line 5)?
8 Why exactly did the aunt dislike the bachelor's story?

Topics for discussion

1   What is the moral (= the lesson) of the bachelor's story?
2   Do you think it's true that children usually like stories about violence? If so, why?
3   Do you like the story? Do you find it funny? Why (not)?
4   What kind of stories did you like when you were a small child?
5   Do you think exposure to violence (in films and stories, or on TV) affects children in any way? If so, how? Do you think there should be more censorship of violent films?

Ray Bradbury
Zero Hour*

*Ray Bradbury is one of the best-known American writers of
science fiction. He has produced various collections of short
stories, including* The Golden Apples of the Sun *and* The
Illustrated Man *(from which this story is taken). Among his
longer works is* Fahrenheit 451, *which was made into a very
successful film. 'Zero Hour' is written in Bradbury's
characteristic exclamatory, poetic style. In it, the classical
science-fiction theme of invasion from space is given a new and
rather frightening twist.*

Oh, it was to be so jolly! What a game! Such excitement
they hadn't known in years. The children catapulted*
this way and that across the green lawns, shouting at
each other, holding hands, flying in circles, climbing
trees, laughing. Overhead the rockets flew, and beetle
cars whispered by on the streets, but the children played
on. Such fun, such tremulous joy, such tumbling and
hearty screaming.

Mink ran into the house, all dirt and sweat. For her
seven years she was loud and strong and definite. Her
mother, Mrs Morris, hardly saw her as she yanked out
drawers and rattled pans and tools into a large sack.

'Heavens, Mink, what's going on?'

'The most exciting game ever!' gasped Mink, pink-
faced.

'Stop and get your breath,' said the mother.

'No, I'm all right,' gasped Mink. 'Okay I take these things, Mom?'

'But don't dent* them,' said Mrs Morris.

'Thank you, thank you!' cried Mink, and boom! she was gone, like a rocket.

Mrs Morris surveyed the fleeing tot.* 'What's the name of the game?'

'Invasion!' said Mink. The door slammed.

In every yard on the street children brought out knives and forks and pokers and old stovepipes and can-openers.

It was an interesting fact that this fury and bustle* occurred only among the younger children. The older ones, those ten years and more, disdained* the affair and marched scornfully off on hikes* or played a more dignified version of hide-and-seek on their own.

Meanwhile, parents came and went in chromium beetles. Repairmen came to repair the vacuum elevators in houses, to fix fluttering television sets or hammer upon stubborn food-delivery tubes. The adult civilization passed and repassed the busy youngsters, jealous of the fierce energy of the wild tots, tolerantly amused at their flourishings,* longing to join in themselves.

'This and this and *this*,' said Mink, instructing the others with their assorted spoons and wrenches.* 'Do that, and bring *that* over here. No! *Here*, ninny!* Right. Now, get back while I fix this.' Tongue in teeth, face wrinkled in thought. 'Like that. See?'

'Yayyyy!' shouted the kids.

Twelve-year-old Joseph Connors ran up.

'Go away,' said Mink straight at him.

'I wanna play,' said Joseph.

'Can't!' said Mink.

'Why not?'

'You'd just make fun of us.'

'Honest, I wouldn't.'

'No. We know *you*. Go away or we'll kick you.'

Another twelve-year-old boy whirred by on little motor skates. 'Hey, Joe! Come on! Let them sissies* play!'

Joseph showed reluctance and a certain wistfulness.* 'I *want* to play.' he said.

'You're old,' said Mink firmly.

'Not *that* old,' said Joe sensibly.

'You'd only laugh and spoil the Invasion.'

The boy on the motor skates made a rude lip noise. 'Come on, Joe! Them and their fairies! Nuts!'*

Joseph walked off slowly. He kept looking back, all down the block.

Mink was already busy again. She made a kind of apparatus with her gathered equipment. She had appointed another little girl with a pad and pencil to take down notes in painful slow scribbles.* Their voices rose and fell in the warm sunlight.

All around them the city hummed. The streets were lined with good green and peaceful trees. Only the wind made a conflict across the city, across the country, across the continent. In a thousand other cities there were trees and children and avenues, business men in their quiet offices taping their voices, or watching televisors. Rockets hovered* like darning needles in the blue sky. There was the universal, quiet conceit* and easiness of men accustomed to peace, quite certain there would never be trouble again. Arm in arm, men all over earth were a united front. The perfect weapons were held in equal trust by all nations. A situation of incredibly beautiful balance had been brought about. There were no traitors among men, no unhappy ones, no disgruntled ones;*

therefore the world was based upon a stable ground. Sunlight illuminated half the world and the trees drowsed* in a tide of warm air.

Mink's mother, from her upstairs window, gazed down.

The children. She looked upon them and shook her head. Well, they'd eat well, sleep well, and be in school on Monday. Bless their vigorous* little bodies. She listened.

Mink talked earnestly to someone near the rose bush – though there was no one there.

These odd children. And the little girl, what was her name? Anna? Anna took notes on a pad. First, Mink asked the rose-bush a question, then called the answer to Anna.

'Triangle,' said Mink.

'What's a tri,' said Anna with difficulty, 'angle?'

'Never mind,' said Mink.

'How you spell it?' asked Anna.

'T-r-i——' spelled Mink slowly, then snapped,* 'Oh, spell it yourself!' She went on to other words. 'Beam,' she said.

'I haven't got tri,' said Anna, 'angle down yet!'

'Well, hurry, hurry!' cried Mink.

Mink's mother leaned out of the upstairs window. 'A-n-g-l-e,' she spelled down at Anna.

'Oh, thanks, Mrs Morris,' said Anna.

'Certainly,' said Mink's mother and withdrew, laughing, to dust the hall with an electro-duster magnet.

The voices wavered* on the shimmery* air. 'Beam,' said Anna. Fading.*

'Four-nine-seven-A-and-B-and-X,' said Mink, far away, seriously. 'And a fork and a string and a – hex-hex-agony – hexagon*al*!'

At lunch Mink gulped milk at one toss and was at the door. Her mother slapped the table.

'You sit right back down,' commanded Mrs Morris. 'Hot soup in a minute.' She poked a red button on the kitchen butler,* and ten seconds later something landed with a bump in the rubber receiver. Mrs Morris opened it, took out a can with a pair of aluminium holders, unsealed* it with a flick,* and poured hot soup into a bowl.

During all this Mink fidgeted.* 'Hurry, Mom! This is a matter of life and death! Aw—'

'I was the same way at your age. Always life and death. I know.'

Mink banged away at the soup.

'Slow down,' said Mom.

'Can't,' said Mink. 'Drill's waiting for me.'

'Who's Drill? What a peculiar name,' said Mom.

'You don't know him,' said Mink.

'A new boy in the neighbourhood?' asked Mom.

'He's new all right,' said Mink. She started on her second bowl.

'Which one is Drill?' asked Mom.

'He's around,' said Mink, evasively.* 'You'll make fun. Everybody pokes fun.* Gee, darn.'*

'Is Drill shy?'

'Yes. No. In a way. Gosh, Mom, I got to run if we want to have the Invasion!'

'Who's invading what?'

'Martians invading Earth. Well, not exactly Martians. They're – I don't know. From up.' She pointed with her spoon.

'And *inside*,' said Mom, touching Mink's feverish brow.

Mink rebelled. 'You're laughing! You'll kill Drill and everybody.'

'I didn't mean to,' said Mom. 'Drill's a Martian?'

'No. He's – well – maybe from Jupiter or Saturn or Venus. Anyway, he's had a hard time.'

'I imagine.' Mrs Morris hid her mouth behind her hand.

'They couldn't figure a way to attack Earth.

'We're impregnable,'* said Mom in mock seriousness.

'That's the word Drill used! Impreg—— That was the word, Mom.'

'My, my, Drill's a brilliant little boy. Two-bit words.'*

'They couldn't figure a way to attack, Mom. Drill says – he says in order to make a good fight you got to have a new way of surprising people. That way you win. And he says also you got to have help from your enemy.'

'A fifth column,' said Mom.

'Yeah. That's what Drill said. And they couldn't figure a way to surprise Earth or get help.'

'No wonder. We're pretty darn strong.' Mom laughed, cleaning up. Mink sat there, staring at the table, seeing what she was talking about.

'Until, one day,' whispered Mink melodramatically, 'they thought of children!'

'*Well!*' said Mrs Morris brightly.

'And they thought of how grown-ups are so busy they never look under rose bushes or on lawns!'

'Only for snails and fungus.'

'And then there's something about dim-dims.'

'Dim-dims?'

'Dimens-shuns.'

'Dimensions?'

'Four of 'em! And there's something about kids under nine and imagination. It's real funny to hear Drill talk.'

Mrs Morris was tired. 'Well, it must be funny. You're keeping Drill waiting now. It's getting late in the day and, if you want to have your Invasion before your sup-per bath, you'd better jump.'

'Do I have to take a bath?' growled Mink.

'You do! Why is it children hate water? No matter what age you live in children hate water behind the ears!'

'Drill says I won't have to take baths,' said Mink.

'Oh, he does, does he?'

'He told all the kids that. No more baths. And we can stay up till ten o'clock and go to two televisor shows on Saturday 'stead of one!'

'Well, Mr Drill better mind his p's and q's.* I'll call up his mother and——'

Mink went to the door. 'We're having trouble with guys like Pete Britz and Dale Jerrick. They're growing up. They make fun. They're worse than parents. They just won't believe in Drill. They're so snooty, 'cause they're growing up. You'd think they'd know better. They were little only a coupla years ago. I hate them worst. We'll kill them *first*.'

'Your father and me last?'

'Drill says you're dangerous. Know why? 'Cause you don't believe in Martians! They're going to let *us* run the world. Well, not just us, but the kids over in the next block, too. I might be queen.' She opened the door.

'Mom?'

'Yes?'

'What's lodge-ick?'

'Logic? Why, dear, logic is knowing what things are true and not true.'

'He *mentioned* that,' said Mink. 'And what's im-pres-sion-able?'* It took her a minute to say it.

'Why, it means——' Her mother looked at the floor, laughing gently. 'It means – to be a child, dear.'

'Thanks for lunch!' Mink ran out, then stuck her

head back in. 'Mom, I'll be sure you won't be hurt much, really!'

'Well, thanks,' said Mom.

Slam went the door.

At four o'clock the audio-visor buzzed. Mrs Morris flipped the tab.* 'Hello, Helen!' she said in welcome.

'Hello, Mary. How are things in New York?'

'Fine. How are things in Scranton? You look tired.'

'So do you. The children. Underfoot,' said Helen.

Mrs Morris sighed. 'My Mink too. The super-Invasion.'

Helen laughed. 'Are your kids playing that game too?'

'Lord, yes. Tomorrow it'll be geometrical jacks* and motorized hopscotch.* Were we this bad when we were kids in '48?'

'Worse. Japs and Nazis. Don't know how my parents put up with me. Tomboy.'*

'Parents learn to shut their ears.'

A silence.

'What's wrong, Mary?' asked Helen.

Mrs Morris's eyes were half closed; her tongue slid slowly, thoughtfully, over her lower lip. 'Eh?' She jerked. 'Oh, nothing. Just thought about *that*. Shutting ears and such. Never mind. Where were we?'

'My boy Tim's got a crush on* some guy named – *Drill*, I think it was.'

'Must be a new password. Mink likes him too.'

'Didn't know it had got as far as New York. Word of mouth, I imagine. Looks like a scrap drive.* I talked to Josephine and she said her kids – that's in Boston – are wild on this new game. It's sweeping the country.'

At this moment Mink trotted into the kitchen to gulp a glass of water. Mrs Morris turned. 'How're things going?'

'Almost finished,' said Mink.

'Swell,'* said Mrs Morris. What's *that?*'

'A yo-yo,'* said Mink. 'Watch.'

She flung the yo-yo down its string. Reaching the end
it——

It vanished.

'See?' said Mink. 'Ope!' Dibbling her finger, she made
the yo-yo reappear and zip up the string.

'Do that again,' said her mother.

'Can't. Zero hour's five o'clock. 'Bye!' Mink exited,
zipping her yo-yo.

On the audio-visor, Helen laughed. 'Tim brought one
of those yo-yos in this morning, but when I got curious
he said he wouldn't show it to me, and when I tried to
work it, finally, it wouldn't work.'

'You're not *impressionable*,' said Mrs Morris.

'What?'

'Never mind. Something I thought of. Can I help you,
Helen?'

'I wanted to get that black-and-white cake recipe——'

The hour drowsed by. The day waned.* The sun lowered
in the peaceful blue sky. Shadows lengthened on the
green lawns. The laughter and excitement continued.
One little girl ran away, crying. Mrs Morris came out
the front door.

'Mink, was that Peggy Ann crying?'

Mink was bent over in the yard, near the rosebush.
'Yeah. She's a scarebaby. We won't let her play, now.
She's getting too old to play. I guess she grew up all of a
sudden.'

'Is that why she cried? Nonsense. Give me a civil*
answer, young lady, or inside you come!'

Mink whirled in consternation,* mixed with irritation. 'I can't quit now. It's almost time. I'll be good. I'm sorry.'

'Did you hit Peggy Ann?'

'No, honest. You ask her. It was something – well, she's just a scaredy pants.'

The ring of children drew in around Mink where she scowled* at her work with spoons and a kind of square-shaped arrangement of hammers and pipes. 'There and there,' murmured Mink.

'What's wrong?' said Mrs Morris.

'Drill's stuck. Half-way. If we could only get him all the way through it'd be easier. Then all the others could come through after him.'

'Can I help?'

'No'm, thanks. I'll fix it.'

'All right. I'll call you for your bath in half an hour. I'm tired of watching you.'

She went in and sat in the electric relaxing chair, sipping a little beer from a half-empty glass. The chair massaged her back. Children, children. Children and love and hate, side by side. Sometimes children loved you, hated you – all in half a second. Strange children, did they ever forget or forgive the whippings* and the harsh, strict words of command? She wondered. How can you ever forget or forgive those over and above you, those tall and silly dictators?

Time passed. A curious, waiting silence came upon the street, deepening.

Five o'clock. A clock sang softly somewhere in the house in a quiet musical voice: 'Five o'clock – five o'clock. Time's a-wasting. Five o'clock,' and purred away into silence.

Zero hour.

Mrs Morris chuckled in her throat. Zero hour.

A beetle car hummed into the driveway. Mr Morris. Mrs Morris smiled. Mr Morris got out of the beetle, locked it, and called hello to Mink at her work. Mink ignored him. He laughed and stood for a moment watching the children. Then he walked up the front steps.

'Hello, darling.'

'Hello, Henry.'

She strained forward on the edge of the chair, listening. The children were silent. Too silent.

He emptied his pipe, refilled it. 'Swell day. Makes you glad to be alive.'

Buzz.

'What's that?' asked Henry.

'I don't know.' She got up suddenly, her eyes widening. She was going to say something. She stopped it. Ridiculous. Her nerves jumped. 'Those children haven't anything dangerous out there, have they?' she said.

'Nothing but pipes and hammers. Why?'

'Nothing electrical?'

'Heck, no,' said Henry. 'I looked.'

She walked to the kitchen. The buzzing continued. 'Just the same, you'd better go tell them to quit. It's after five. Tell them——' Her eyes widened and narrowed. 'Tell them to put off their Invasion until tomorrow.' She laughed, nervously.

The buzzing grew louder.

'What are they up to? I'd better go look, all right.'

The explosion!

The house shook with dull sound. There were other explosions in other yards on other streets.

Involuntarily, Mrs Morris screamed. 'Up this way!' she cried senselessly, knowing no sense, no reason. Perhaps she saw something from the corners of her eyes; perhaps she smelled a new odour or heard a new noise.

There was no time to argue with Henry to convince him. Let him think her insane.* Yes, insane! Shrieking, she ran upstairs. He ran after her to see what she was up to.* 'In the attic!' she screamed. 'That's where it is!' It was only a poor excuse to get him in the attic in time. Oh, God – in time!

Another explosion outside. The children screamed with delight, as if at a great fireworks* display.

'It's not in the attic!' cried Henry. 'It's outside!'

'No, no!' Wheezing,* gasping, she fumbled* at the attic door. 'I'll show you. Hurry! I'll show you!'

They tumbled into the attic. She slammed the door, locked it, took the key, threw it into a far, cluttered* corner.

She was babbling* wild stuff now. It came out of her. All the subconscious suspicion and fear that had gathered secretly all afternoon and fermented* like a wine in her. All the little revelations and knowledges and sense that had bothered her all day and which she had, logically and carefully and sensibly, rejected and censored. Now it exploded in her and shook her to bits.

'There, there,' she said, sobbing against the door. 'We're safe until tonight. Maybe we can sneak out. Maybe we can escape!'

Henry blew up too, but for another reason. 'Are you crazy? Why'd you throw that key away? Damn it, honey!'

'Yes, yes, I'm crazy, if it helps, but stay here with me!'

'I don't know how in hell I *can* get out!'

'Quiet. They'll hear us. Oh, God, they'll find us soon enough——'

Below, them, Mink's voice. The husband stopped. There was a great universal humming and sizzling,* a screaming and giggling.* Downstairs the audio-televisor buzzed and buzzed insistently, alarmingly, violently. *Is that Helen calling?* thought Mrs Morris. *And is she calling about what I think she's calling about?*

Footsteps came into the house. Heavy footsteps.

'Who's coming in my house?' demanded Henry angrily. 'Who's tramping around down there?'

Heavy feet. Twenty, thirty, forty, fifty of them. Fifty persons crowding into the house. The humming. The giggling of the children. 'This way!' cried Mink, below.

'Who's downstairs?' roared Henry. 'Who's there?'

'Hush. Oh, nonononononono!' said his wife weakly, holding him. 'Please, be quiet. They might go away.'

'Mom?' called Mink. 'Dad?' A pause. 'Where are you?'

Heavy footsteps, heavy, heavy, very *heavy* footsteps, came up the stairs. Mink leading them.

'Mom?' A hesitation. 'Dad?' A waiting, a silence.

Humming. Footsteps towards the attic. Mink's first.

They trembled together in silence in the attic, Mr and Mrs Morris. For some reason the electric humming, the queer cold light suddenly visible under the door crack, the strange odour and the alien* sound of eagerness in Mink's voice finally got through to Henry Morris too. He stood, shivering, in the dark silence, his wife beside him.

'Mom! Dad!'

Footsteps. A little humming sound. The attic-lock melted. The door opened. Mink peered inside, tall blue shadows behind her.

'Peekaboo,'* said Mink.

Ray Bradbury

Glossary

page 55
zero hour: the time when an attack is planned to start
catapulted: flew

page 56
dent: damage
tot: small child
bustle: busy activity
disdained: were contemptuous of
hikes: long country walks
flourishings: complicated movements
wrenches: kind of tools
ninny: idiot (children's slang)

page 57
sissies: silly babies (children's slang)
wistfulness: sadness
nuts: mad
scribbles: childish writing
hovered: stayed in the air without moving
conceit: feeling of self-satisfaction
disgruntled ones: people who felt they had been treated
　　unfairly

page 58
drowsed: half slept
vigorous: strong and energetic
snapped: said angrily
wavered: shook
shimmery: trembling with heat
fading: growing quieter

page 59
butler: servant
unsealed: opened
flick: quick movement
fidgeted: moved restlessly

evasively : avoiding answering the question
make fun, poke fun : laugh at him, not take him seriously
Gee, darn : an exclamation

page 60
impregnable : impossible to defeat
two-bit words : big, important words (two bits = a quarter of a
   dollar)

page 61
mind his p's and q's : be careful about his behaviour
impressionable : deeply affected by what one sees and hears

page 62
flipped the tab : moved the switch
jacks, hopscotch : traditional children's games
tomboy : girl who likes boys' games
got a crush on : got a childish passion for
scrap drive : collection of useless pieces of old metal

page 63
swell : wonderful
yo-yo : child's toy – a wheel that goes up and down on a string
waned : moved towards its end
civil : polite
consternation : shock

page 64
scowled : frowned angrily
whippings : beatings

page 66
insane : mad
up to : doing
fireworks : small explosives used at celebrations
wheezing : breathing noisily
fumbled at the attic door : tried to open it with unsteady hands
cluttered : untidy, full of rubbish
babbling : talking quickly in a confused way

Ray Bradbury

fermented: developed
sizzling: burning noise
giggling: childish laughter

page 67
alien: strange and foreign
peekaboo: word used in children's games (when a child looks
  out of a hiding-place)

Questions

1 What things in the story show that it takes place in the
   future? What sort of society do people live in?
2 What sort of child is Mink?
3 What exactly were Mink and her friends doing with the
   pieces of metal they collected?
4 Who was Drill?
5 Why did the invaders choose younger children to help
   them?
6 What do you think an 'audio-visor' is (page 62 line 5)?
7 Why does Mrs Morris become silent and thoughtful when
   her friend says 'Parents learn to shut their ears' (page 62
   line 18)?
8 Why do you think Mink tells her parents what the children
   and the invaders are planning to do?
9 Who are 'those tall and silly dictators' (page 64 line 26)?
10 Why did Mrs Morris say 'I'll show you' to her husband
   (page 66 line 11)?

Topics for discussion

1 The writer presents an unusual and frightening picture of
   children and their attitude to adults. Do you think there
   is any truth in it (even if it's rather exaggerated)? Have
   you read any other stories or seen any films which show
   children in the same light?

2   Mrs Morris wonders if children ever forgive their parents
    for the way they use their authority (page 64 line 25).
    Do you think, in general, parents are too authoritarian
    towards their children? How strict were your parents with
    you? How strict would you be with your own children?

3   Mrs Morris's friend says that 'parents learn to shut their
    ears'; Mrs Morris takes very little interest in Mink's
    disappearing yo-yo. Do you think this is typical of adult
    behaviour towards children? If so, why?

4   Why do you think the author puts the audio-visor
    conversation into the story (page 62)?

5   Do you find the story frightening? Do you like it? Why
    (not)?

6   Can you talk about other science-fiction stories you have
    read, or films you have seen?

Maurice Shadbolt
The People Before

The Maoris, the original inhabitants of New Zealand, were driven off their land by European settlers in the middle of the nineteenth century. The action of this story takes place nearly a century later, after the First World War, on a small farm. The principal character is a tough, hard-working farmer who fights to earn a living for his family from the land to which he is passionately and possessively attached. The crisis of the story comes when he realizes clearly for the first time that 'his' land originally belonged to the Maoris, the 'people before'. The author, Maurice Shadbolt (born in 1932), is a New Zealander; he has published a number of short stories, and works as a film director.

I

My father took on that farm not long after he came back from the first war. It was pretty well the last farm up the river. Behind our farm, and up the river, there was all kind of wild country. Scrub* and jagged* black stumps* on the hills, bush in gullies* where fire hadn't reached; hills and more hills, deep valleys with caves and twisting rivers, and mountains white with winter in the distance. We had the last piece of really flat land up the river. It wasn't the first farm my father'd taken on – and it certainly wasn't to be the last – but it was the most remote. He always said that was why he'd got the place for a song. This puzzled me as a child. For I'd heard, of course, of having to sing for your supper. I wondered what words, to what tune, he was obliged to sing for the farm; and where, and why? Had he travelled up the river, singing a strange song, charming his way into possession of the land? It always perplexed me.

And it perplexed me* because there wasn't much room for singing in my father's life. I can't remember ever having heard him sing. There was room for plodding* his paddocks* in all weathers, milking cows and sending cream down river to the dairy factory, and cursing the bloody government; there was room in his life for all these things and more, but not for singing.

In time, of course, I understood that he only meant he'd bought the place cheaply. Cheaply meant for a song. I couldn't, even then, quite make the connection. It remained for a long while one of those adult mysteries. And it was no use puzzling over it, no use asking my father for a more coherent* explanation.

'Don't be difficult,' he'd say. 'Don't ask so many damn questions. Life's difficult enough, boy, without all your damn questions.'

He didn't mean to be unkind; it was just his way. His life was committed to winning order from wilderness. Questions were a disorderly intrusion,* like gorse* or weed* springing up on good pasture.* The best way was to hack* them down, grub out* the roots, before they could spread. And in the same way as he checked* incipient* anarchy on his land he hoped, perhaps, to check it in his son.

By that time I was old enough to understand a good many of the things that were to be understood. One of them, for example, was that we weren't the first people on that particular stretch of land. Thirty or forty years before, when white men first came into our part of the country, it was mostly forest. Those first people fired the forest, right back into the hills, and ran sheep. The sheep grazed* not only the flat, but the hills which rose sharply behind our farm; the hills which, in our time, had become stubbly* with manuka* and fern.* The flatland had been pretty much scrub too, the day my father first saw it; and the original people had been gone twenty years – they'd given up, or been ruined by the land; we never quite knew the story. The farmhouse stood derelict* among the returning wilderness.

Well, my father saw right away that the land – the flat land – was a reasonable proposition for a dairy farm. There was a new launch* service down to the nearest dairy factory, in the township ten miles away; only in the event of flood, or a launch breakdown, would he have to dispose of his cream by carrying it on a sledge* across country, three miles, to the nearest road.

So he moved in, cleared the scrub, sowed new grass, and brought in cows. Strictly speaking, the hills at the back of the farm were his too, but he had no use for them. They made good shelter from the westerlies.* Otherwise he never gave the hills a thought, since he had all the land he could safely manage; he roamed* across them after wild pig, and that was about all. There were bones up there, scattered skeletons of lost sheep, in and about the scrub and burnt stumps.

Everything went well; he had the place almost paid off by the time of the depression.* 'I never looked back, those years,' he said long afterwards. It was characteristic of him not to look back. He was not interested in who had the farm before him. He had never troubled to inquire. So far as he was concerned, history only began the day he first set foot on the land. It was his, by sweat and legal title; that was all that mattered. That was all that could matter.

He had two boys; I was the eldest son. 'You and Jim will take this place over one day,' he often told me. 'You'll run it when I get tired.'

But he didn't look like getting tired. He wasn't a big man, but he was wiry* and thin with a lean face and cool blue eyes; he was one of those people who can't keep still. When neighbours called he couldn't ever keep comfortable in a chair, just sitting and sipping tea, but had to start walking them round the farm – or at least the male neighbours – pointing out things here and there. Usually work he'd done, improvements he'd made: the new milking-shed, the new water-pump on the river. He didn't strut* or boast,* though; he just pointed them out quietly, these jobs well done. He wanted others to share his satisfaction. There was talk of electricity coming through to the farm, the telephone; a road up the river was scheduled.* It would all put the value of the property up. The risk he'd taken on the remote and abandoned land seemed justified in every way.

He didn't ever look like getting tired. It was as if he'd been wound up* years before, like something clockwork, and set going: first fighting in the war, then fighting with the land; now most of the fighting was done, he sometimes found it quite an effort to keep busy. He never took a holiday. There was talk of taking a holiday, one winter when the cows dried off; talk of us all going down to the sea, and leaving a neighbour to look after the place. But I don't think he could have trusted anyone to look after his land, not even for a week or two in winter when the cows were dried off. Perhaps, when Jim and I were grown, it would be different. But not until. He always found some reason for us not to get away. Like our schooling.

'I don't want to interfere with their schooling,' he said once. 'They only get it once in their lives. And they might as well get it while they can. I didn't get much. And, by God, I regret it now. I don't know much, and I might have got along all right, but I might have got along a damn sight better* if I'd had more schooling. And I'm not going to interfere with theirs by carting them off for a holiday in the middle of the year.'

Yet even then I wondered if he meant a word of it, if he really wasn't just saying that for something to say. He was wrangling* at the time with my mother, who held opinions on a dwindling* number of subjects. She never surrendered any of these opinions, exactly; she just kept them more and more to herself until, presumably, they lapsed* quietly and died. As she herself, much later, was to lapse quietly from life, without much complaint.

For if he'd really been concerned about our schooling, he might have been more concerned about the way we fell asleep in afternoon classes. Not that we were the only ones. Others started getting pretty ragged* in the afternoons too. A lot of us had been up helping our fathers since early in the morning. Jim and I were up at half-past four most mornings to help with the milking and working the separators.* My father increased his herd year after year, right up to the depression. After school we rode home just in time for the evening milking. And by the time we finished it was getting dark; in winter it was dark by the time we were half-way through the herd.

I sometimes worried about Jim looking worn in the evenings, and I often chased him off inside before milking was finished. I thought Jim needed looking after; he wasn't anywhere near as big as me. I'd hear him scamper* off to the house, and then I'd set about* stripping* the cows he had left. Father sometimes complained.

'You'll make that brother of yours a softy,' he said. 'The boy's got to learn what work means.'

'Jim's all right,' I answered. 'He's not a softy. He's just not very big. That's all.'

He detested softies, even the accomplices* of softies. My mother, in a way, was such an accomplice. She'd never been keen about first me, then Jim, helping with work on the farm. But my father said he couldn't afford to hire a man to help with the herd. And he certainly couldn't manage by himself, without Jim and me.

'Besides,' he said, 'my Dad and me used to milk two hundred cows' – sometimes, when he became heated, the number rose to three hundred – 'when I was eight years old. And thin as a rake too, I was. Eight years old and thin as a rake. It didn't do me no harm. You boys don't know what work is, let me tell you.'

So there all argument finished. My mother kept one more opinion to herself.

And I suppose that, when I chased Jim off inside, I was only taking my mother's side in the argument, and was only another accomplice of softies. Anyway, it would give me a good feeling afterwards – despite anything my father would have to say – when we tramped* back to the house, through the night smelling of frost or rain, to find Jim sitting up at the table beside my mother while she ladled out* soup under the warm yellow lamplight. He looked as if he belonged there, beside her; and she always looked, at those times, a little triumphant. Her look seemed to say that one child of hers, at least, was going to be saved from the muck* of the cowshed. And I suppose that was the beginning of how Jim became his mother's boy.

I remained my father's. I wouldn't have exchanged him for another father. I liked seeing him with people, a man among men. This happened on winter Saturdays when we rode to the township for the football. We usually left Jim behind to look after my mother. We tethered our horses near the football field and went off to join the crowd. Football was one of the few things which interested my father outside the farm. He'd been a fine rugby forward in his day and people respected what he had to say about the game. He could out-argue most people; probably out-fight them too, if it ever came to that. He often talked about the fights he'd had when young. For he'd done a bit of boxing too, only he couldn't spare the time from his father's farm to train properly. He knocked me down once, with his bare fists, in the cowshed; and I was careful never to let it happen again. I just kept my head down for days afterwards, so that he wouldn't see the bruises on my face or the swelling round my eye.

At the football he barracked* with the best of them in the thick of the crowd. Sometimes he called out when the rest of the crowd was silent and tense;* he could be very sarcastic* about poor players, softies who were afraid to tackle* properly.

After the game he often called in, on the way home, to have a few beers with friends in the township's sly-grog shop* – we didn't have a proper pub in the township – while I looked after the horses outside. Usually he'd find time, while he gossiped* with friends, to bring me out a glass of lemonade. At times it could be very cold out there, holding the horses while the winter wind swept round, but it would be nice to know that I was remembered. When he finished we rode home together for a late milking. He would grow talkative, as we cantered* towards dark, and even give me the impression he was glad of my company. He told me about the time he was young, what the world looked like when he was my age. His father was a sharemilker, travelling from place to place; that is, he owned no land of his own and did other people's work.

'So I made up my mind, boy,' he told me as we rode along together, 'I made up my mind I'd never be like that. I'd bend my head to no man. And you know what the secret of that is, boy? Land. Land of your own. You're independent, boy. You can say no to the world. That's if you got your own little kingdom. I reckon it was what kept me alive, down there on the beach at Gallipoli,* knowing I'd have some land I could call my own.' This final declaration seemed to dismay him* for some reason or other, perhaps because he feared he'd given too much of himself away. So he added half-apologetically, 'I had to think of something, you know, while all that shooting was going on. They say it's best to fix your mind on something if you don't want to be afraid. That's what I fixed my mind on, anyhow. Maybe it did keep me alive.'

In late winter or spring we sometimes arrived back, on Saturdays, to see the last trembling light of sunset fade from the hills and land. We'd canter along a straight stretch, coast* up a rise, rein in* the horses, and there it was – his green kingdom, his tight tamed acres beneath the hills and beside the river, a thick spread of fenced grass from the dark fringe of hill-scrub down to the ragged* willows* above the water. And at the centre was his castle, the farmhouse, with the sheds scattered round, and the pine trees.

Reining in on that rise, I knew, gave him a good feeling. It would also be the time when he remembered all the jobs he'd neglected, all the work he should have done

79

instead of going to the football. His conscience would keep him busy all day Sunday.

At times he wondered – it was a conversation out loud with himself – why he didn't sell up and buy another place. There were, after all, more comfortable farms, in more convenient locations nearer towns or cities. 'I've built this place up from nothing,' he said. 'I've made it pay, and pay well. I've made this land worth something. I could sell out for a packet.* Why don't I?'

He never really – in my presence anyway – offered himself a convincing explanation. Why didn't he? He'd hardly have said he loved the land: loved, in any case, would have been an extravagance.* Part of whatever it was, I suppose, was the knowledge that he'd built where someone else had failed; part was that he'd given too much of himself there, to be really free anywhere else. It wouldn't be the same, walking on to another successful farm, a going concern, everything in order. No, this place – this land from the river back up to the hills – was his. In a sense it had only ever been his. That was why he felt so secure.

If Sunday was often the day when he worked hardest, it was also the best day for Jim and me, our free day. After morning milking, and breakfast, we did more or less what we liked. In summer we swam down under the river-willows; we also had a canoe tied there and some-times we paddled* up-river, under great limestone bluffs* shaggy* with toi toi,* into country which grew wilder and wilder. There were huge bearded caves in the bush above the water which we explored from time to time. There were also big eels* to be fished from the pools of the river.

As he grew older Jim turned more into himself, and became still quieter. You could never guess exactly what he was thinking. It wasn't that he didn't enjoy life; he just had his own way of enjoying it. He didn't like being with his father, as I did; I don't even know that he always enjoyed being with me. He just tagged along* with me: we were, after all, brothers. When I was old enough, my father presented me with a .22 rifle; Jim never showed great enthusiasm for shooting. He came along with me, all right, but he never seemed interested in the rabbits or wild goat I shot, or just missed. He wandered around the hills, way behind me, entertaining himself and collecting things. He gathered leaves, and tried to identify the plants from which the leaves came. He also collected stones, those of some interesting shape or texture;* he had a big collection of stones. He tramped along, in his slow, quiet way, poking into* everything, adding to his collections. He wasn't too slow and quiet at school, though; he was faster than most of us with an answer. He borrowed books from the teacher, and took them home. So in time he became even smarter with his answers. I grew to accept his difference from most people. It didn't disturb me particularly: on the farm he was still quiet, small Jim. He was never too busy with his books to come along with me on Sundays.

There was a night when Jim was going through some new stones he'd gathered. Usually, in the house, my father didn't take much notice of Jim, his reading or his hobbies. He'd fought a losing battle for Jim, through the years, and now accepted his defeat. Jim still helped us with the herd, night and morning, but in the house he was ignored. But this night my father went across to the table and picked up a couple of new stones. They were greenish, both the same triangular shape.

'Where'd you get these?' he asked.

Jim thought for a moment; he seemed pleased by the interest taken in him. 'One was back in the hills,' he said. 'The other was in a cave up the river. I just picked them up.'

'You mean you didn't find them together?'

'No,' Jim said.

'Funny,' my father said. 'They look like greenstone. I seen some greenstone once. A joker* found it, picked it up in the bush. Jade,* it is; same thing. This joker sold it in the city for a packet. Maori stuff. Some people'll buy anything.'

We all crossed to the table and looked down at the greenish stones. Jim's eyes were bright with excitement.

'You mean these used to belong to the Maoris?' he said. 'These stones?'

'Must have,' my father said. 'Greenstone doesn't come natural round here. You look it up in your books and you'll see. Comes from way down south, near the mountains and glaciers.* Had to come up here all the way by canoe. They used to fight about greenstone, once.' He paused and looked at the stones again. 'Yes,' he added. 'I reckon that's greenstone, all right. You never know, might be some money in that stuff.'

Money was a very important subject in our house at that time. It was in a lot of households, since that time was the depression. In the cities they were marching in the streets and breaking shop windows. Here on the farm it wasn't anywhere near so dramatic. The grass looked much the same as it had always looked; so did the hills and river. All that had happened, really, was that the farm had lost its value. Prices had fallen; my father sometimes wondered if it was worth while sending cream to the factory. Some of the people on poorer land, down the river, had walked off their properties. Everything was tighter. We had to do without new clothes, and there wasn't much variety in our eating. We ran a bigger garden, and my father went out more frequently shooting wild pig for meat. He had nothing but contempt for the noisy people in the city, the idlers* and wasters who preferred to go shouting in the streets rather than fetch a square meal for their families, as he did with his rifle. He thought they, in some way, were to blame for the failure of things. Even so, he became gripped by the idea that he might have failed himself, somehow; he tried to talk himself out of this idea – in my presence – but without much success. Now he had the land solid beneath his feet, owned it entirely, it wasn't much help at all. If it wasn't for our garden and the wild pig, we might starve. The land didn't bring him any money; he might even have to leave it. He had failed, perhaps much as the land's former owners had failed; why? He might have answered the question for himself satisfactorily, while he grubbed away at the scrub encroaching on* our pasture; but I doubt it.

'Yes,' he said. 'Might be some money in that stuff.'

But Jim didn't seem to hear, or understand. His eyes were still bright. 'That means there must have been Maoris here in the old days,' he said.

'I suppose there must have,' my father agreed. He didn't seem much interested. Maoris were Maoris. There weren't many around our part of the river; they were mostly down towards the coast. (Shortly after this, Jim did some research and told me the reason why. It turned out that the land about our part of the river had been confiscated* from them after the Maori wars.) 'They were most places, weren't they?' he added.

'Yes,' Jim said. 'But I mean they must have been here. On our place.'

'Well, yes. They could of been. Like I said, they were most places.' It didn't seem to register as particularly important. He picked up the greenstones again. 'We ought to find out about this,' he continued. 'There might be a bit of money in it.'

Later Jim took the stones to school and had them identified as Maori adzes.* My father said once again that perhaps there was money in them. But the thing was, where to find a buyer? It mightn't be as easy as it used to be. So somehow it was all forgotten. Jim kept the adzes.

Jim and I did try to find again that cave in which he had picked up an adze. We found a lot of caves, but none of them seemed the right one. Anyway we didn't pick up another adze. We did wander down one long dripping cave, striking matches, and in the dark tripped on something. I struck another match and saw some brownish-looking bones. 'A sheep,' I said. 'It must have come in here and got lost.'

Jim was silent; I wondered why. Then I saw he wasn't looking at the bones, but at a human skull* propped* on a ledge of the cave. It just sat there sightless, shadows dancing in its sockets.*

We got out of that cave quickly. We didn't even talk about it when we reached home. On the whole I preferred going out with my .22 after rabbits.

2

It was near the end of the depression. But we didn't know that then, of course. It might have been just the beginning, for all we knew. My father didn't have as much interest in finishing jobs as he used to have. He tired easily. He'd given his best to the land, and yet his best still wasn't good enough. There wasn't much sense in anything, and his dash* was done. He kept going out of habit.

I'd been pulled out of school to help with the farm. Jim still more or less went to school. I say more or less because he went irregularly. This was because of sickness. Once he was away in hospital two months. And of course it cost money; my father said we were to blame, we who allowed Jim to become soft and sickly. But the doctor thought otherwise; he thought Jim had been worked hard enough already. And when Jim returned to the farm he no longer helped with the herd. And this was why I had to leave school: if he couldn't have both of us working with him part-time, my father wanted one full-time. Jim was entirely surrendered at last, to the house and his books, to school and my mother. I didn't mind working on the farm all day, with my father; it was, after all, what I'd always wanted. All the same, I would have been happier if he had been: his doubts about himself, more and more frequently expressed, disturbed me. It wasn't like my father at all. He was convinced now he'd done the wrong thing, somewhere. He went back through the years, levering* each year up like a stone, to see what lay beneath; he never seemed to find anything. It was worst of all in winter, when the land looked bleak*, the hills were grey with low cloud, and the rain swirled* out of the sky. All life vanished from his face and I knew he detested* everything: the land which had promised him independence was now only a muddy snare;* he was bogged* here, between hills and river, and couldn't escape. He had no pride left in him for the place. If he could have got a price for the farm he would have gone. But there was no longer any question of a

85

Maurice Shadbolt

price. He could walk off if he liked. Only the bush would claim it back.

It was my mother who told us there were people coming. She had taken the telephone message while we were out of the house, and Jim was at school.

'Who are they?' my father said.

'I couldn't understand very well. It was a bad connection. I think they said they were the people who were here before.'

'The people who were here before? What the hell do they want here?' His eyes became suspicious under his frown.

'I think they said they just wanted to have a look around.'

'What the hell do they want here?' my father repeated, baffled.* 'Nothing for them to see. This farm's not like it was when they were here. Everything's different. I've made a lot of changes. They wouldn't know the place. What do they want to come back for?'

'Well,' my mother sighed, 'I'm sure I don't know.'

'Perhaps they want to buy it,' he said abruptly; the words seemed simultaneous with* his thought, and he stiffened with astonishment. 'By God, yes. They might want to buy the place back again. I hadn't thought of that. Wouldn't that be a joke? I'd sell, all right – for just about as much as I paid for the place. I tell you, I'd let it go for a song, for a bloody song. They're welcome.'

'But where would we go?' she said, alarmed.

'Somewhere,' he said. 'Somewhere new. Anywhere.'

'But there's nowhere,' she protested. 'Nowhere any better. You know that.'

'And there's nowhere any worse,' he answered. 'I'd start again somewhere. Make a better go of things.'

'You're too old to start again,' my mother observed softly.

There was a silence. And in the silence I knew that what my mother said was true. We all knew it was true.

'So we just stay here,' he said. 'And rot. Is that it?' But he really wished to change the subject. 'When are these people coming?'

'Tomorrow, I think. They're staying the night down in the township. Then they're coming up by launch.'

'They didn't say why they were interested in the place?'

'No. And they certainly didn't say they wanted to buy it. You might as well get that straight now. They said they just wanted a look around.'

'I don't get it. I just don't get it. If I walked off this place I wouldn't ever want to see it again.'

'Perhaps they're different,' my mother said. 'Perhaps they've got happy memories of this place.'

'Perhaps they have. God knows.'

It was early summer, with warm lengthening days. That sunny Saturday morning I loitered* about the house with Jim, waiting for the people to arrive. Eventually, as the sun climbed higher in the sky, I grew impatient and went across the paddocks to help my father. We were working together when we heard the sound of the launch coming up the river.

'That's them,' he said briefly. He dropped his slasher* for a moment, and spat on his hands. Then he took up the slasher again and chopped* into a new patch of unruly* gorse.

I was perplexed. 'Well,' I said, 'aren't you going down to meet them?'

'I'll see them soon enough. Don't worry.' He seemed to be conducting an argument with himself as he hacked into the gorse. 'I'm in no hurry. No. I'm in no hurry to see them.'

I just kept silent beside him.

'Who are they, anyway?' he went on. 'What do they want to come traipsing* round my property for? They've got a bloody cheek.'*

The sound of the launch grew. It was probably travelling round the last bend in the river now, past the swamp* of raupo,* and banks prickly with flax* and toi toi. They were almost at the farm. Still chopping jerkily,* my father tried to conceal his unease.

'What do they want?' he asked for the last time. 'By God, if they've come to gloat,* they've got another think coming. I've made something decent out of this place, and I don't care who knows it.'

He had tried everything in his mind and it was no use: he was empty of explanation. Now we could see the launch white on the gleaming river. It was coasting up the bank. We could also see people clustered* on board.

'Looks like a few of them,' I observed. If I could have done so without upsetting my father, I would have run down to meet the launch, eager with curiosity. But I kept my distance until he finished arguing with himself.

'Well,' he said, as if he'd never suggested otherwise, 'we'd better go down to meet them, now they're here.' He dug his slasher into the earth and began to stalk* off down to the river. I followed him. His quick strides soon took him well ahead of me; I had to run to keep up.

· · ·

Then we had our surprise. My father's step faltered;* I blundered* up alongside him. We saw the people climbing off the launch. And we saw who they were, at last. My father stopped perfectly still and silent. They were

Maoris. We were still a hundred yards or more away, but there was no mistaking their clothing and colour. They were Maoris, all right.

'There's something wrong somewhere,' he said at last. 'It doesn't make sense. No Maori ever owned this place. I'd have known. Who the hell do they think they are, coming here?'

I couldn't answer him. He strode on down to the river. There were young men, and two old women with black headscarves. And last of all there was something the young men carried. As we drew nearer we saw it was an old man in a rough litter.* The whole party of them fussed over making the old man comfortable. The old women, particularly; they had tattoos* on their chins and wore shark-tooth necklaces. They straightened the old man's blankets and fixed the pillow behind his head. He had a sunken, withered* face and he didn't look so much sick, as tired. His eyes were only half-open as everyone fussed around. It looked as if it were a great effort to keep them that much open. His hair was mostly grey, and his dry flesh sagged* in thin folds about his ancient neck. I reckoned that he must have been near enough to a hundred years old. The young men talked quickly among themselves as they saw my father approaching. One came forward, apparently as spokesman. He looked about the oldest of them, perhaps thirty. He had a fat, shiny face.

'Here,' said my father. 'What's all this about?' I knew his opinion of Maoris: they were lazy, drank too much, and caused trouble. They just rode on the backs of the men on the land, like the loafers* in the cities. He always said we were lucky there were so few in our district. 'What do you people think you're doing here?' he demanded.

'We rang up yesterday,' the spokesman said. 'We told your missus* we might be coming today.'

'I don't know about that. She said someone else was coming. The people who were here before.'

'Well,' said the young man, smiling. 'We were the people before.'

'I don't get you. You trying to tell me you owned this place?'

'That's right. We owned all the land around this end of the river. Our tribe.'

'That must have been a hell of a long time ago.'

'Yes,' agreed the stranger. 'A long time.' He was pleasantly spoken and patient. His round face, which I could imagine looking jolly, was very solemn just then.

I looked around and saw my mother and Jim coming slowly down from the house.

'I still don't get it,' my father said. 'What do you want?'

'We just want to go across your land, if that's all right. Look, we better introduce ourselves. My name's Tom Taikaka. And this is——'

My father was lost in a confusion of introductions. But he still didn't shake anyone's hand. He just stood his ground, aloof* and faintly hostile.* Finally there was the old man. He looked as though he had gone to sleep again.

'You see he's old,' Tom explained. 'And has not so long to live. He is the last great man of our tribe, the oldest. He wishes to see again where he was born. The land over which his father was chief. He wishes to see this before his spirit departs for Rerengawairua.'*

By this time my mother and Jim had joined us. They were as confused as we were.

'You mean you've come just to——' my father began.

'We've come a long way,' Tom said. 'Nearly a hundred miles, from up the coast. That's where we live now.'

'All this way. Just so——'

'Yes,' Tom said. 'That's right.'

'Well,' said my father. 'What do you know?* What do you know about that?' Baffled, he looked at me, at my mother, and even finally at Jim. None of us had anything to say.

'I hope we're not troubling you,' Tom said politely. 'We don't want to be any trouble. We just want to go across your land, if that's all right. We got our own tucker* and everything.'

We saw this was true. The two old women had large flax kits of food.

'No liquor?' my father said suspiciously. 'I don't want any drinking round my place.'

'No,' Tom replied. His face was still patient. 'No liquor. We don't plan on any drinking.'

The other young men shyly agreed in the background. It was not, they seemed to say, an occasion for drinking.

'Well,' said my father stiffly, 'I suppose it's all right. Where are you going to take him?' He nodded towards the old sleeping man.

'Just across your land. And up to the old *pa*.'*

'I didn't know there used to be any *pa* round here.'

'Well,' said Tom. 'It used to be up there.' He pointed out the largest hill behind our farm, one that stood well apart and above the others. We called it Craggy* Hill, because of limestone outcrops.* Its flanks* and summit* were patchy with tall scrub. We seldom went near it, except perhaps when out shooting; then we circled its steep slopes rather than climbed it. 'You'd see the terraces,' Tom said, 'if it wasn't for the scrub. It's all hidden now.'

Now my father looked strangely at Tom. 'Hey,' he said, 'you sure you aren't having me on?* How come you know that hill straight off?* You ever been here before?'

'No,' Tom said. His face shone as he sweated with the effort of trying to explain everything. 'I never been here before. I never been in this part of the country before.'

'Then how do you know that's the hill, eh?'

'Because,' Tom said simply, 'the old men told me. They described it so well I could find the place blindfold.* All the stories of our tribe are connected with that hill. That's where we lived, up there, for hundreds of years.'

'Well, I'll be damned. What do you know about that?' My father blinked, and looked up at the hill again. 'Just up there, eh? And for hundreds of years.'

'That's right.'

'And I never knew. Well, I'll be damned.'

'There's lots of stories about that hill,' Tom said. 'And a lot of battles fought round here. Over your place.'

'Right over my land?'

'That's right. Up and down here, along the river.'

My father was so astonished he forgot to be aloof. He was trying to fit everything into his mind at once – the hill where they'd lived hundreds of years, the battles fought across his land – and it was too much.

'The war canoes would come up here,' Tom went on. 'I reckon they'd drag them up somewhere here' – he indicated the grassy bank on which we were standing – 'in the night, and go on up to attack the *pa* before sunrise. That's if we hadn't sprung a trap for them down here. There'd be a lot of blood soaked into this soil.' He kicked at the earth beneath our feet. 'We had to fight a long while to keep this land here, a lot of battles. Until there was a day when it was no use fighting any more. That was when we left.'

We knew, without him having to say it, what he meant. He meant the day when the European took the land. So we all stood quietly for a moment. Then my mother spoke.

'You'd better come up to the house,' she said. 'I'll make you all a cup of tea.'

A cup of tea was her solution to most problems.

We went up to the house slowly. The young men followed behind, carrying the litter. They put the old man in the shade of a tree, outside the house. Since it seemed the best thing to do, we all sat around him; there wouldn't have been room for everyone in our small kitchen anyway. We waited for my mother to bring out the tea.

Then the old man woke. He seemed to shiver, his eyes opened wide, and he said something in Maori. 'He wonders where he is,' Tom explained. He turned back to the old man and spoke in Maori.

He gestured, he pointed. Then the old man knew. We all saw it the moment the old man knew. It was as if we were all willing him towards that moment of knowledge. He quivered* and tried to lift himself weakly; the old women rushed forward to help him. His eyes had a faint glitter* as he looked up to the place we called Craggy Hill. He did not see us, the house, or anything else. Some more Maori words escaped him in a long, sighing rush. '*Te Wahiokoahoki*,' he said.

'It is the name,' Tom said, repeating it. 'The name of the place.'

The old man lay back against the women, but his eyes were still bright and trembling. They seemed to have a life independent of his wrinkled* flesh. Then the lids came down, and they were gone again. We could all relax.

'*Te Wahiokoahoki*,' Tom said. 'It means the place of

93

happy return. It got the name when we returned there after our victories against other tribes.'

My father nodded. 'Well, I'll be damned,' he said. 'That place there. And I never knew.' He appeared quite affable* now.

My mother brought out tea. The hot cups passed from hand to hand, steaming and sweet.

'But not so happy now, eh?' Tom said. 'Not for us.'

'No. I don't suppose so.'

Tom nodded towards the old man. 'I reckon he was just about the last child born up there. Before we had to leave. Soon there'll be nobody left who lived there. That's why they wanted young men to come back. So we'd remember too.'

Jim went into the house and soon returned. I saw he carried the greenstone adzes he'd found. He approached Tom shyly.

'I think these are really yours,' he said, the words an effort.

Tom turned the adzes over in his hand. Jim had polished them until they were a vivid green. 'Where'd you get these, eh?' he asked.

Jim explained how and where he'd found them. 'I think they're really yours,' he repeated.

There was a brief silence. Jim stood with his eyes downcast, his treasure surrendered. My father watched anxiously; he plainly thought Jim a fool.

'You see,' Jim added apologetically, 'I didn't think they really belonged to anyone. That's why I kept them.'

'Well,' Tom said, embarrassed. 'That's real nice of you. Real nice of you, son. But you better keep them, eh? They're yours now. You find, you keep. We got no claims here any more. This is your father's land now.'

Then it was my father who seemed embarrassed. 'Leave me out of this,' he said sharply. 'You two settle it between you. It's none of my business.'

'I think you better keep them all the same,' Tom said to Jim.

Jim was glad to keep the greenstone, yet a little hurt by rejection of his gift. He received the adzes back silently.

'I tell you what,' Tom went on cheerfully, 'you ever find another one, you send it to me, eh? Like a present. But you keep those two.'

'All right,' Jim answered, clutching the adzes. He seemed much happier. 'I promise if I find any more, I'll send them to you.'

'Fair enough,' Tom smiled, his face jolly. Yet I could see that he too really wanted the greenstone.

After a while they got up to leave. They made the old man comfortable again and lifted him. 'We'll see you again tomorrow,' Tom said. 'The launch will be back to pick us up.'

'Tomorrow?' my father said. It hadn't occurred to him that they might be staying overnight on his land.

'We'll make ourselves a bit of a camp up there tonight,' Tom said, pointing to Craggy Hill. 'We ought to be comfortable up there. Like home, eh?' The jest* fell mildly* from his lips.

'Well, I suppose that's all right.' My father didn't know quite what to say. 'Nothing you want?'

'No,' Tom said. 'We got all we want, thanks. We'll be all right. We got ourselves. That's the important thing, eh?'

We watched them move away, the women followed by the young men with the litter. Tom went last, Jim trotting* along beside him. They seemed, since the business

95

of the greenstone, to have made friends quickly. Tom appeared to be telling Jim a story.

I thought for a moment that my father might call Jim back. But he didn't. He let him go.

The old women now, I noticed, carried green foliage.* They beat it about them as they walked across our paddocks and up towards Craggy Hill; they were chanting* or singing, and their wailing* sound came back to us. Their figures grew smaller with distance. Soon they were clear of the paddocks and beginning to climb.

My father thumbed back his hat and rubbed a handkerchief across his brow. 'Well, I'll be damned,' he said.

. . .

We sat together on the porch* that evening, as we often did in summer after milking and our meal. Yet that evening was very different from any other. The sun had set, and in the dusk* we saw faint smoke rising from their campfire on Craggy Hill, the place of happy return. Sometimes I thought I heard the wailing sound of the women again, but I couldn't quite be sure.

What were they doing up there, what did they hope to find? We both wondered and puzzled, yet didn't speak to each other.

Jim had returned long before, with stories. It seemed he had learned, one way and another, just about all there was to be learned about the tribe that had once lived on Craggy Hill. At the dinner table he told the stories breathlessly. My father affected* to be not much interested; and so, my father's son, did I. Yet we listened, all the same.

'Then there was the first musket,'* Jim said. 'The first musket in this part of the country. Someone bought it from a trader down south and carried it back to the *pa*.

Another tribe, one of their old enemies, came seeking *uta* – *uta* means revenge – for something that had been done to them the year before. And when they started climbing up the hill they were knocked off one by one, with the musket. They'd never seen anything like it before. So the chief of the tribe on Craggy Hill made a sign of peace and called up his enemies. It wasn't a fair fight, he said, only one tribe with a musket. So he'd let his enemies have the musket for a while. They would have turns with the musket, each tribe. He taught the other tribe how to fire and point the musket. Then they separated and started the battle again. And the next man to be killed by the musket was the chief's eldest son. That was the old man's uncle – the old man who was here today.'

'Well, I don't know,' said my father. 'Sounds bloody queer to me. That's no way to fight a battle.'

'That's the way they fought,' Jim maintained.*

So we left Jim, still telling stories to my mother, and went out on the porch.

The evening thickened. Soon the smoke of the campfire was lost. The hills grew dark against the pale sky. and at last my father, looking up at the largest hill of all, spoke softly . . .

'I suppose a man's a fool,' he said. 'I should never have let that land go. Shouldn't ever have let it go back to scrub. I could have run a few sheep up there. But I just let it go. Perhaps I'll burn it off one day, run a few sheep. Sheep might pay better too, the way things are now.'

But it wasn't, somehow, quite what I expected him to say. I suppose he was just trying to make sense of things in his own fashion.

3

They came down off Craggy Hill the next day. The launch had been waiting for them in the river some time.

When we saw the cluster of tiny figures, moving at a fair pace* down the hills, we sensed there was something wrong. Then, as they drew nearer, approaching us across the paddocks, we saw what was wrong. There was no litter, no old man. They all walked freely, separately. They were no longer burdened.*

Astonished, my father strode up to Tom. 'Where is he?' he demanded.

'We left him back up there,' Tom said. He smiled sadly and I had a queer feeling that I knew exactly what he would say.

'Left him up there?'

'He died last night, or this morning. When we went to wake him he was cold. So we left him up there. That's where he wanted to be.'

'You can't do that,' my father protested. 'You can't just leave a dead man like that. Leave him anywhere. And, besides, it's my land you're leaving him on.'

'Yes,' Tom said. 'Your land.'

'Don't you understand? You can't just leave dead people around. Not like that.'

'But we didn't just leave him around. We didn't just leave him anywhere. We made him all safe and comfortable. He's all right. You needn't worry.'

'Christ, man,' my father said. 'Don't you see?'

But he might have been asking a blind man to see. Tom just smiled patiently and said not to worry. Also he said they'd better be catching the launch. They had a long way to go home, a tiring journey ahead.

And as he walked off, my father still arguing beside him, the old women clashed* their dry greenery, wailing, and their shark-tooth necklaces danced under their heaving throats.

In a little while the launch went noisily off down the river. My father stood on the bank, still yelling after them. When he returned to the house, his voice was hoarse.*

He had a police party out, a health officer too. They scoured* the hills, and most of the caves they could find. They discovered no trace of a burial, nor did they find anything in the caves. At one stage someone foolishly suggested we might have imagined it all. So my father produced the launchman and people from the township as witness to the fact that an old Maori, dying, had actually been brought to our farm.

That convinced them. But it didn't take them anywhere near finding the body. They traced* the remnants* of the tribe, living up the coast, and found that indeed an old man of the tribe was missing. No one denied that there had been a visit to our farm. But they maintained that they knew nothing about a body. The old man, they said, had just wandered off into the bush; they hadn't found him again.

He might, they added, even still be alive. Just to be on the safe side, in case there was any truth in their story, the police put the old man on the missing persons register, for all the good that might have done.

But we knew. We knew every night we looked up at the hills that he was there, somewhere.

So he was still alive, in a way. Certainly it was a long time before he let us alone.

And by then my father had lost all taste for the farm.

It seemed the land itself had heaped some final indignity upon him, made a fool of him. He never talked again, anyway, about running sheep on the hills.

When butter prices rose and land values improved, a year or two afterwards, he had no hesitation in selling out. We shifted* into another part of the country entirely, for a year or two, and then into another. Finally we found ourselves milking a small herd for town supply, not far from the city. We're still on that farm, though there's talk of the place being purchased soon for a city sub-division. We think we might sell, but we'll face the issue* when it arises.

Now and then Jim comes to see us, smart in a city suit, a lecturer at the university. My father always found it difficult to talk to Jim, and very often now he goes off to bed and leaves us to it. One thing I must say about Jim: he has no objection to helping with the milking. He insists that he enjoys it; perhaps he does. It's all flat-land round our present farm, with one farm much like another, green grass and square farmhouses and pine shelter belts,* and it's not exactly the place to sit out on a summer evening and watch shadows gathering on the hills. Because there aren't hills within sight; or shadows either, for that matter. It's all very tame and quiet, apart from cars speeding on the highway.

I get on reasonably well with Jim. We read much the same books, have much the same opinions on a great many subjects. The city hasn't made a great deal of difference to him. We're both married, with young families. We also have something else in common: we were both in the war, fighting in the desert. One evening after milking, when we stood smoking and yarning* in the cool, I remembered something and decided I might put a question to Jim.

'You know,' I began, 'they say it's best, when you're under fire in the war, to fix your mind on something remote. So you won't be afraid. I remember Dad telling me that. I used to try. But it never seemed any good. I couldn't think of anything. I was still as scared* as hell.'

'I was too. Who wasn't?'

'But I mean, did you ever think of anything?'

'Funny thing,' he said. 'Now I come to think of it, I did. I thought of the old place – you know, the old place by the river. Where,' he added, and his face puckered* into a grin, 'where they buried that old Maori. And where I found those greenstones. I've still got them at home, you know, up on the mantelpiece. I seem to remember trying to give them away once, to those Maoris. Now I'm glad I didn't. It's my only souvenir from there, the only thing that makes that place still live for me.' He paused. 'Well, anyway, that's what I thought about. That old place of ours.'

I had a sharp pain. I felt the dismay of a long-distance runner who, coasting confidently to victory, imagining himself well ahead of the field, finds himself overtaken and the tape* snapped* at the very moment he leans forward to breast it. For one black moment it seemed I had been robbed of something which was rightfully mine.

I don't think I'll ever forgive him.

Glossary

page 72

scrub : small trees and bushes

jagged : with sharp points

stumps : the pieces left in the ground after trees have fallen or been cut down

gullies : places where water runs down a hillside

page 73
it perplexed me: I couldn't understand it
plodding: walking heavily (across)
paddocks: small grass fields
coherent: logical
intrusion: something that disturbs
gorse: a bush with yellow flowers and sharp thorns
weed: unwanted plants
pasture: grassland
hack: cut
grub out: dig out
checked: stopped
incipient: beginning

page 74
grazed: ate grass
stubbly: rough
manuka: a tree that grows in New Zealand
fern: a plant
derelict: abandoned, left empty
launch: river boat
sledge: car that runs on strips of metal or wood instead of
    wheels
westerlies: westerly winds
roamed: wandered
depression: economic crisis

page 75
wiry: tough
strut: walk proudly
boast: praise himself
scheduled: planned
wound up: you wind up the spring of a watch or clock to make
    it go

page 76
a damn sight better: a lot better (slang)
wrangling: arguing
dwindling: getting smaller

lapsed: dropped
ragged: unable to work efficiently, disorganized
separators: machines for separating cream from milk

page 77
scamper: run with small steps
set about: start
stripping: milking
accomplices: helpers (of people who do something wrong)
tramped: walked slowly and heavily
ladled out: served with a ladle (= a very big spoon)
muck: dirt

page 78
tethered: tied up
barracked: shouted at the players
tense: the opposite of relaxed
sarcastic: unpleasantly ironic
tackle: try to take the ball away from another player
sly-grog shop: illegal drinking house (New Zealand slang)
gossiped: chatted
cantered: rode at a slow gallop

page 79
Gallipoli: English name for Gelibolu, a town on the
    Dardanelles strait in Turkey, where Australian and New
    Zealand soldiers attacked, and were badly defeated, in the
    First World War
dismay him: make him unhappy
coast: ride (or drive) slowly and easily
rein in: stop
ragged: untidy
willows: kind of trees

page 80
a packet: a lot of money (slang)
extravagance: exaggerated, over-emotional expression
paddled: a canoe is pushed along with paddles
bluffs: cliffs

shaggy: hairy
toi toi: a bush that grows in New Zealand
eels: long thin fish that look like snakes

page 81
tagged along with: followed
texture: the way something feels when you touch it
poking into: examining, investigating

page 82
joker: chap (New Zealand slang)
jade: a valuable stone
glaciers: rivers of ice

page 83
idlers: lazy people
encroaching on: invading
confiscated: taken away

page 84
adzes: tools used for shaping wood
skull: head bone
propped: supported, leaning
sockets: eye holes

page 85
dash: energy, enthusiasm
levering: lifting
bleak: cold
swirled: came blown on the wind
detested: hated
snare: trap
bogged: stuck

page 86
baffled: unable to understand
simultaneous with: at the same time as

page 87
loitered: stood around doing nothing

slasher: tool for cutting plants
chopped: cut
unruly: undisciplined

page 88
traipsing: walking (the word expresses anger at the people who
 are walking)
they've got a bloody cheek: they haven't got any respect for other
 people (slang)
swamp: very wet soft land
raupo: a plant that grows in New Zealand
flax: a plant
jerkily: irregularly
gloat: show satisfaction over my failure
clustered: grouped
stalk: walk proudly
faltered: hesitated
blundered: walked clumsily, unsteadily

page 89
litter: bed that can be carried
tattoos: patterns made by pricking the skin with a needle and
 putting in ink or dyes (tattooing was a Maori custom)
withered: dried up, very old-looking
sagged: hung loosely
loafers: people who don't work
missus: wife

page 90
aloof: cold and separate
hostile: unfriendly
Rerengawairua: in the Maori religion, the world where spirits
 go after death

page 91
What do you know?: exclamation expressing surprise
tucker: food (New Zealand slang)
pa: meeting house in old Maori village
craggy: rocky

Maurice Shadbolt

outcrops : big rocks sticking out of the ground
flanks : sides
summit : top
having me on : telling me lies (slang)

page 92
straight off : immediately
blindfold : with my eyes covered

page 93
quivered : trembled
glitter : expression of excitement
wrinkled : full of lines

page 94
affable : friendly

page 95
jest : joke
mildly : gently
trotting : running slowly

page 96
foliage : leafy branches
chanting : singing on one note
wailing : crying noisily
porch : covered doorway
dusk : evening half-light
affected : pretended
musket : early kind of rifle

page 97
maintained : insisted

page 98
at a fair pace : quite fast
burdened : loaded

page 99
clashed: beat
hoarse: rough from shouting
scoured: searched thoroughly
traced: found
remnants: rest

page 100
shifted: moved
issue: problem, question
pine shelter belts: lines of pine trees planted to give protection
   from the wind
yarning: telling stories

page 101
scared: frightened
puckered: puckers are lines or folds in the skin
tape: the piece of tape which marks the end of a race
snapped: broken

Questions

1 How did the boys' father manage to buy the farm so
   cheaply?
2 'I could sell out for a packet. Why don't I?' (page 80
   line 9). Why do you think he didn't?
3 What exactly is meant by 'He'd fought a losing battle for
   Jim, through the years' (page 81 line 27)?
4 Explain 'They were marching in the streets and breaking
   shop windows' (page 82 line 26).
5 Why didn't the land bring the boys' father any money
   (page 83 line 15)?
6 Compare the attitudes of Jim and his father to the
   greenstone adzes.
7 Who did the father first think that the 'people before'
   were?
8 Why was he worried and nervous about their coming to
   his farm?

9 What is surprising about his saying 'No Maori ever owned this place' (page 89 line 5)?
10 'That must have been a hell of a long time ago' (page 90 line 9). About how long?
11 Why did the Maoris want to come to the farm? Did they tell the boys' father the exact truth about this?
12 What is the joke when Tom says 'Like home, eh?' (page 95 line 24)?

Topics for discussion

1 What sort of person is the father in the story?
2 Compare the personalities of the two boys.
3 What kind of relationship does the father have with his sons? What do you feel about his attitude to each of them?
4 What is the father's attitude to the past? How does this change as the story develops?
5 What attitudes do the two brothers, their father, and the Maoris have to the land? Why do you think the father wished that he had cleared the hills and put sheep on them, after the Maoris' visit? Why was he furious when he learnt there was a dead Maori on his land? What effect did this have on him? In what way did the land 'make a fool of him' (page 100, line 2)? Explain the last sentence of the story.
6 What attitude does the father have towards Maoris in general? Can you think of any other countries where there are people in the same position as the New Zealand Maoris? How have the people in the other countries been treated in the past, and how are they treated now?
7 Do you like the story? Why (not)?

Joyce Cary
The Breakout

*Joyce Cary (1888–1957) came from an Anglo–Irish family.
After studying art, he began a career in the Colonial Political
Service in Nigeria. Ill-health forced him to give this up, and he
became a writer, producing several successful novels as well as
short stories and books on art. In 'The Breakout' Cary deals
with the problem of a middle-aged man who realizes that all his
relationships are empty and false. He tries to break out, but the
pessimistic ending suggests that there is no real escape.*

Tom Sponson, at fifty-three, was a thoroughly successful
man. He had worked up a first-class business, married a
charming wife, and built himself a good house in the
London suburbs that was neither so modern as to be pretentious* nor so conventional as to be dull. He had good
taste. His son, Bob, nineteen, was doing well at Oxford;
his daughter, April, aged sixteen, who was at a good
school, had no wish to use make-up, to wear low frocks,
or to flirt. She still regarded herself as too young for these
trifling* amusements. Yet she was gay, affectionate, and
thoroughly enjoyed life. All the same, for some time Tom
had been aware that he was working very hard for very
little. His wife, Louie, gave him a peck* in the morning
when he left for the office and, if she were not at a party,
a peck in the evening when he came home. And it was
obvious that her life was completely filled with the child-

ren, with her clothes, with keeping her figure slim, with keeping the house clean and smart, with her charities, her bridge, her tennis, her friends, and her parties.

The children were even more preoccupied – the boy with his own work and his own friends, the girl with hers. They were polite to Tom, but if he came into the room when they were entertaining a friend, there was at once a feeling of constraint.* Even if they were alone together, he perceived that when he came upon them they were slightly embarrassed, and changed the subject of their conversation, whatever it was. Yet they did not seem to do this when they were with their mother. He would find them all three, for instance, laughing at something, and when he came in they would stop laughing and gaze at him as if he had shot up through the floor. In fact, if he asked what the joke was his wife would say, 'You wouldn't understand' or 'Nothing' or 'I'll tell you afterwards', but she never did tell him afterwards; she would put him off with some remark like, 'Oh, it's perfectly silly, about something April said.'

He said to himself, 'It isn't only that they don't need me, but I'm a nuisance to them. I'm in the way. I'm superfluous.'* One morning when he was just going to get into his car and his wife had come out to say good-bye, he suddenly made an excuse, saying, 'Just a moment, I've left a letter', and went back to his desk, and then dashed out to the car and drove off, pretending to forget that good-bye had not been said.

Immediately he felt that he could not stand any more of this existence; it was nonsense. It was not as though his wife and children were depending any more on the business; he could sell it to a combine* tomorrow, and it would support all of them in comfort. Actually he would miss the business; it was his chief interest. But if he had to give it up for the sake of freedom, of a break in this senseless life, he could do even that. Yes, joyfully.

As he circled Trafalgar Square, that is to say, as he came within the last few hundred yards from his office, he told himself that he could not go on. It was as though that moment when he dodged* the customary good-bye had broken a contact. The conveyor belt* on which his life had been caught up had stopped as if at a short circuit,* a break in a switch. No, he could not go on. So, instead of turning down the Strand out of the Square, he drove straight on to a West End garage.

An hour later, he was in the train for Westford, a seaside place where he had once spent a summer holiday before his marriage, with three friends from college. On the luggage rack was a new suitcase containing new pyjamas, shoes, a new kit,* as for a holiday by the sea – even new paperbacks for a wet day.

It was February, but when he reached Westford he was surprised, for a moment, to find that both its hotels were closed. Only the village pub, The Case Is Altered, was still open for visitors, and as he sat in the coffee-room, he appeared to be the only visitor, except for a commercial traveller, one Sims, a dignified* young man who addressed him with the most formal politeness and showed a strong tendency to talk politics – politics on what he called the 'highest level'.

In his view, he said, what parliaments did and what dictators talked about did not really matter; what mattered was population statistics and economics. 'You can put over* anything with the wireless and the telly – that's the way these dictators do it – but you can't feed people on words. They'll swallow all the lies you like, but they can't live on hot air.* Sooner or later most of these chaps have to face facts.'

'Yes,' said Tom. 'A lot later – generally too late. Look at what Hitler did with his little yarn* – and called it the Big Lie all the time. Look at all the people eating lies now and getting poison all the time. What can they do, poor devils ? So long as the big noise* has a really tough police.'

Tom was a Liberal, a strong supporter of the United Nations. A week before, he had been saying just the same things as Mr Sims; probably they had come out of the same papers. But now all at once he was revolted,* quite furious with Mr Sims, with all those nice chaps at the club and the golf course, who had been so ready to talk this nonsense with him, who simply refused to face facts, especially the enormous, obvious fact that civilization was going to smash just because of all this cant,* this wangling,* this political gabble,* this nonsense.

Mr Sims shook his head and remarked that the police hadn't saved the Tsar.

'No,' Tom said. 'What knocked him out was a superior brand of cant. He thought the people loved him, and sent his Guards to the front.* But the Bolshies* told the people they'd bring in the golden age right off.* And they won. They had a bigger lie and they were smarter swindlers.* The poor old Tsar only cheated himself; they cheated everybody.'

Suddenly Tom caught Mr Sims's eye fixed upon him with a speculative* alarm. The man was shocked. He was so used to the regular nonsense, to the old, worn records grinding out* the same old popular tune, that he was bewildered by this contradiction.

'Quite a new idea,' Mr Sims murmured. 'Very interesting.' He was growing more and more alarmed.

'Excuse me,' Tom muttered, and hurried out into the front hall. It was almost a run. He was afraid of losing his temper with Mr Sims, who was obviously a nice chap, a very nice chap, who read all the best papers, the best nonsense.

What especially angered him in Mr Sims was that Mr Sims's nonsense was his own nonsense of a week before. Sims was a looking-glass in which he saw his own silly face. And it made it no better that, as he now perceived, he had always known his nonsense to be nonsense. All that time when he had been talking it at business luncheons, at the club, in the train, at breakfast to his own family, he had had the same deep feeling: My God, what nonsense!

For years he had been hiding this knowledge, just as he had always pretended that he enjoyed nothing so much as his family life. How often had he boasted of the sympathetic devotion of his wife and children, saying how lucky he was compared with so many others, who found themselves ciphers* in their own homes. Why, why had he gone on telling himself these lies, living a life of hypocrisy?* It was as if he had been drugged – or was it simply that the air was so thick with nonsense, with cant, that it was almost impossible for any man to see the truth, even the biggest, the most obvious truth? Wasn't it simply by a stroke of luck that he had broken out into clear air? And as if the words themselves demanded the action, he put on his mackintosh* and went out.

It was raining still, but the opposite side of the bay was sharp and clear, as though seen through a lens. The grey sky was brilliant with diffused* light, and the breeze had a taste of sea salt. The whole world seemed washed as clean as the pebbles* on the beach.

He walked along the front.* Westford's great charm in the old days had been its smallness, its lack of enterprise.* Apart from the two hotels, both old-fashioned, and even forbidding* to strangers, there were only a dozen or so boarding-houses along the front, and almost the entire town was in the twenty or so buildings facing the sea, and in the main street of the old village branching off at right angles. There was what was called a Marine Parade, but it was simply a paved path along the front road with, on the seaward side, a strip of rough grass where half a dozen seats had been provided. Below, the magnificent beach had neither pier* nor bathing huts. The great landlord who owned Westford was against huts, and summer visitors were expected to use tents that they could hire from the town council. There were no municipal* gardens, bandstands,* putting* courses, or sideshows to vulgarize* the place, which, apart from the absence of bathing machines,* might have been existing still in the eighteen-sixties.

The wind was rising and big waves were thumping* on the beach. The sea turned almost black, and the wet fronts of the houses, in spite of their gay colours, began to have a dreary* look. The town seemed absolutely empty; not a human being was in sight. The only living creature to be seen was a dog with its nose in the gutter* – as Tom appeared from around a corner, it jumped and looked at him, uttered one sharp bark, and cantered* away, completely shocked by the intrusion.* But the very dreariness of the scene, the monotonous pounding* of the waves, the hiss of the rain in the pools, gave Tom the kind of pleasure that one gets from the defiance* of an enemy. He was stimulated, excited. He felt his strength; he felt that he had done well. He had made a big decision and saved his life, and he went down to the beach and walked up and down close to the waves until the rain grew heavy. His shoes filled with sand and he remembered that he had only one suit with him. He turned back to the pub, intending to read one of his new crime novels.

In the little hall of the private entrance, the clerk, who was also the barman, was waiting for him with the register, and, upon an impulse that, for the moment, he did not understand and did not examine, he hesitated and then wrote down the name Charles Stone and gave a false address. He was surprised at himself – he detested* such trickery – but it was only twenty minutes later that, lying upstairs on his bed with his book, he realized how necessary it had been, how wisely he had followed his impulse. 'In the first excitement,' he said to himself, 'they might well ask the B.B.C. or the newspapers to start a hunt; the last thing I want is any publicity. I'll write to Louie at once and get things settled in a sensible manner.'

That evening – in fact, as soon as he could, with decent politeness, separate himself from Mr Sims, who was anxious to make him realize that if you can fool the people, you can't fool population statistics, so long, of course, as they are reliable* – he slipped off to his room to write to Louie. There was no writing-table in the room, or any provision for writing, so he set his new suit-case on his knee and proceeded to draft* a letter on the flyleaf* of his paper-back.

'Darling Louie', he began, but stopped immediately. He had always written 'Darling Louie', but how could he begin a letter of farewell, an ultimatum* proposing an end to their marriage, with 'Darling Louie'? He crossed it out and wrote 'My dear Louie'. This also struck him as false. She was not his dear Louie. And was he going to start a new life of truth, of sincerity, by writing this criminal lie? 'Dear So-and-so.' What hundreds of letters to total strangers, to touts,* to frauds* and crooks,* to people who were, in fact, absolutely detestable to him, he had started with this lying formula, this stereotyped* nonsense. Louie was simply the woman who lived in his house, like a creature dropped from Mars, more strange to him than any stranger. A woman whom he supported and who had no real contact with him at all, who did not even speak the same language. He began again, without preamble:* I dare say you wonder where I am, but it does not really matter. As far as you and the children are concerned, I have not existed anywhere for a long time. I'm not blaming anyone for this state of affairs. I imagine it's a very common one for married couples in our situation. The children are practically grown up and don't need us any more; they certainly have not needed me for years past, and your life is entirely full of your own private interests. For a long time, I have been aware that I was only in the way. You would be much happier, much freer, as a widow. You could make one of those marriages that women in their forties do make after their children cease to need them, a marriage with a man suited to the new woman you have become. There is something to be said for a change of partners at our age. After all, people don't stop growing and changing simply because they are married. I agree that they have a duty to their children, but when that duty has been discharged* it is absurd* to make them waste the rest of their lives in pretending to a community* of interests which they no longer possess. It's even bad for the children, now they are old enough to think for themselves, to live in this atmosphere of fake* and hypocrisy. They get infected,* too, and so the nonsense goes on to another generation.' It was a good letter; he was surprised how good it was. He realized that it expressed for him feelings that had been present for years, and that he had been, unnoticed by himself, collecting all kinds of information bearing on* his argument. It was a good letter, but he did not send it that evening. He had no notepaper or envelopes with

him. He could not make a fair copy and he was not sure
that he had not said too much. The whole thing, as read
through, had a somewhat professorial air. It lacked the
conviction that moved him so strongly. It gave no hint
of the bitterness that he felt to be justifiable. He had
been a good husband, a good father, and he could not
help feeling that he had been treated with ingratitude.
He lay awake half the night thinking of new things that
he could put in this letter. Once he even turned on the
light to write a phrase in another of his crime novels.

Next day he rewrote the letter. It was not till Thurs-
day, three days after his flight, that he went out in the
town to seek notepaper and envelopes. Then he found
that the one stationer's had nothing to his taste – only
stationery sets done up in ribbon and containing deckle-
edged* paper of the most vulgar type, or the cheapest
blocks. Both, he felt, were quite impossible for his letter.
He had always been particular about notepaper. However, Westford was only ten miles from the large seaside
town of Lilmouth, and he would enjoy a visit there, too.
He and his college friends had spent a very happy afternoon and evening at Lilmouth at the annual fair. He
called, therefore, at the garage, to hire a car, and found
that there was one that would be available the next day.
He gave the order and returned to the pub. He was in
no hurry to write his letter. Why, Louie knew that he
was all right. He had phoned the office to tell them that
he had to go away for a while, that he would send his
address in due course,* and he had asked them to inform
his wife.

A letter from or to Louie would start all sorts of trouble,
and meanwhile he was only just beginning to enjoy his
new life. He had found out how to dodge Mr Sims –
simply by having his meals earlier. And time was passing

far more quickly than he had expected. It was astonishing how this lounging,* thoughtful, careless existence had already fallen into a routine. A late breakfast, a stroll along the front, coffee at eleven in a little café that remained open apparently for the use of unemployed landladies, who came there to discuss their bookings for the next season. Then to the stationer's for the London papers, then early luncheon with the papers to read. After luncheon, a doze* in his room. Then another stroll along the front, or, if it were fine, over the headland* and along the coast for a mile or two. The sea breeze was unequalled for giving one an appetite. He had not for years so much enjoyed either the prospect of dinner or dinner itself. The Case Is Altered did not attempt French cooking. All the better. It provided excellent meat, beer, and cheese, and plenty of them. After dinner he was ready for a pipe and another look at the papers, and then to bed, where he read himself to sleep in a few minutes. Even for luncheon he found that he had an appetite, and he was sniffing the smell of chops in the hall, the smell that not many months before would have turned him away from such a place in the first moment, when a large, dark figure, which seemed to have been waiting in the coffee-room doorway, stepped out and said, 'Mr Sponson?'

Tom, without thought, answered, 'My name is Stone,' and then, indignant* to see himself confronted by a policeman, went on, 'What do you want here? Why should I answer your questions?'

The policeman, a large West Country man with a red face, answered, in a deprecating manner, as if to say 'Excuse me', that he had not asked any questions. He was holding his helmet in front of his stomach in the manner of a shy man who wants to occupy his hands. Tom saw at once that this polite, apologetic manner was merely assumed.* It was hypocritical nonsense.

He said shortly, 'Well, don't, because I don't intend to answer any.'

'That's all right, sir,' said the policeman. 'No offence, I hope.' And he went out. Even his gesture, as, turning the corner, he threw up his chin and replaced his helmet on his head, annoyed Tom. It seemed to carry all that confidence of authority, that calm superiority of power, that is so offensive to the private citizen.

He went upstairs to his room in a rage and began to pack. He must get away at once. What enraged him was the thought that he had been followed, spied upon.* Louie must have gone to the police. What right had they to pursue him like this? He had done no wrong; in fact, he was trying to do the right thing, the sensible thing. No doubt, Louie felt offended; perhaps she was hurt in her pride. She didn't want her friends to know that her marriage had failed. But if there were any publicity now it would be entirely her own fault. He had done everything to avoid publicity. He rang the bell for his bill before he remembered that it did not ring; none of the bells rang. But almost at once a maid, as if summoned by telepathy, appeared. She looked with surprise at his suitcase, half packed, and said that luncheon was ready and that someone was waiting for him.

'Someone waiting?' he demanded. 'Who's waiting?'

'In the coffee-room, sir – a gentleman.'

'What gentleman?'

The maid did not know, and seemed startled by the question. She hurried away almost at a run, and he realized that he had been shouting at her.

Tom banged his suitcase shut. The maid was obviously a spy, just as Mr Sims had certainly been a spy, and all barmen like to keep in with the police. That policeman had certainly talked to the barman, and how had the police got to know about him except from spies in the place? All at once Westford seemed to him almost as loathsome* as his own suburb at home, full of people making demands upon him, thinking about him, discussing him. Certainly everyone in the pub would be discussing him – this mysterious affair, Mr Sponson's disappearance.

And who was this gentleman? Probably a detective. It must be a detective. He took his suitcase with him down the back stairs. He would escape by the yard. But the barman was at the bottom of the stairs, looking up at him with a thoughtful air, and when he turned towards the front hall, there was his brother, Fred. Fred was shaking hands with him before he realized who he was.

'Hullo, old chap, how are you? This is a bit of luck, to find you here,' Fred said.

'What do you mean, find me here? What do you take me for? You've come after me – I suppose Louie sent you?'

'My dear old chap, that's none of my business. It's only that – there's one or two small points about our own family affairs – about some of our father's things.'

Fred was in the Army, a major. Tom and he had always been good friends, but they had no family interests in common except their memories. Fred was married, with three children, the paternal estate* had been divided long ago, and Tom suddenly lost his temper. 'Look, Fred,' he said, 'I don't know how you got on my tracks – I suppose I'm being spied on all the time – but it's no good coming after me like this. You won't get me to go back.'

'My dear chap, I wouldn't dream of it. In fact, I'm

all for this idea of taking a holiday, a real holiday. You've not had a real holiday for years. Why not come ski-ing with me in Norway?' He slapped Tom on the shoulder with a smile that was just a little too hearty,* too brotherly.

Tom pushed the hand from his shoulder. 'Don't talk nonsense,' he said. 'The thing is to humour* the lunatic, isn't it? Go along with the poor chap in his wildest fantods.'*

'Good heavens, no, old boy. I never saw you looking better.'

'Because the fact is that I've just got sane* – for the first time in years. I've just waked up to the kind of imbecile* nonsense that my life had become.'

'Exactly. I couldn't agree more. All work and no play – a real holiday – '

'Of course I want a holiday – for the rest of my life. You think this is a breakdown.* It isn't. It's a breakout. What do you suppose my life is like at home – as they call it? Bob and April stopped being my children years ago when they went away to school, and as for Louie, I often wonder whether she ever has been my real wife. Certainly I've never known just what she was after or what she thought of me. And these last two years I've simply been a nuisance to her. This is a break, in fact, for her as well as for me. It isn't so much a new life we need as a real life. As it is, we just carry on this marriage by habit. It's just an imitation marriage, a robot marriage. We go through the gestures because we've been wound up and can't stop the machinery. Well, now I *have* stopped the machinery and I'm going to have some life on my own and give Louie some life, too. She needn't be afraid she will be left flat.* There's plenty of money for both of us.'

Fred made a face as if to say, 'Really, I don't want all

Joyce Cary

this talk,' and said, 'Quite. I quite see your point, old chap, though, in fact, I gather she's upset, quite ill, they say – But what about some lunch? I'm hungry.' He sat down at a table in the coffee-room and called the waiter.

But Tom was not going to be wangled* in this manner. He wasn't going to have Fred go on pretending that this act of justice and sincerity was a trifle.* He would not even sit down at the table. He bent over it towards Fred and said, 'So she's made herself ill. She would, but why? Because she's upset at what people will say. Because she may have to give up a few parties. Because her routine is changed – like someone who's knocked off* cigarettes and doesn't know how to pass the time.'

The waiter had arrived with Fred's chop, mashed potato, and brussels sprouts, the standard lunch at the pub. Fred took a mouthful and then shouted, 'Waiter, half a can* of old and mild!'*

This affectation* of ease still more irritated Tom. 'You don't believe me,' he said. 'But what do you know about it? I tell you I'm nothing to Louie but a provider and I'm going on providing. That's to say, she'll get exactly the same income as before.'

The waiter came with the beer. Fred took a sip and said, 'Might be worse,' and then, sticking his fork in the chop, remarked, 'The children.'

'Yes, the children. And if I'm nothing much to Louie, I'm still less to the children. They have their own lives, they've had 'em for years.' And when Fred went on eating his chop, Tom, now very exasperated,* began a long speech about the children. He wasn't blaming them, he said. They were nice children. It was, in fact, quite right that they should be having their own lives. What was wrong and perfectly stupid was this pretence that he

122

was needed any more – this hypocrisy, which was just as bad for them as for him, and all for nothing. His own life was simply being wasted for nothing.

Fred still went on eating, and Tom, leaning across the table on his knuckles,* felt like some village orator* addressing a meeting so bored that it cannot even listen. Abruptly he stopped. He was so angry that for a moment he had an impulse to take up Fred's beer and throw it in his face. The impulse was so strong that he hastily turned away and went out of the room, and, catching up his suitcase, hat and coat, made for the door. But before he could escape, the barman popped out* from the saloon bar. 'Your bill, sir.' When he had paid the bill, Fred had picked up the suitcase and was saying, 'Let me give you a hand, old chap. What about the old heart?' Fred carried the suitcase all the way to the bus. He talked of their childhood. Some old album* of photographs had turned up in his attic. Would Tom like to see them? There ought to be a share-out.

Tom said nothing; he could not speak for fear of screaming his rage at Fred. He knew that if he began to speak, if he said a word to him, it would be a shriek, and he dared not shriek.

The bus was standing in front of The Lobster Pot, the village beerhouse, but it was not to leave for half an hour yet. Fred proposed that they should go in for a parting glass, but Tom hastily climbed into the empty bus and took his seat. For a moment he was afraid, he was terrified, that Fred would sit down beside him and go on talking, go on trying to smooth him down, to make him feel that nothing was really wrong, that all this that had happened was quite an ordinary event.

But Fred apparently had more sense, or possibly better instructions. He put down the suitcase beside Tom and held out his hand. 'Well, old chap, I suppose you don't want me here, but if there's anything I can do, I hope you'll send along and let me know.' Tom did not take the hand. He wanted to do so, he was fond of Fred, but it seemed to him now that if he touched his hand he would be acknowledging that Fred's mission was not completely nonsense, that after all there was something in the conventional shibboleth* of family unity that had sent him to Westford. He could not touch his hand, and after a moment Fred said good-bye again and went off. What a relief. Tom felt such a sense of release that he was full of gratitude to his brother. He thought, I must write to him, I must tell him that I didn't want to be rude. It wasn't a personal matter; it was just a question of principle.

That night he was in Liverpool, at a quiet back-street hotel, a commercial hotel. His plan was to go abroad, to Eire or Europe. He had sent to the office for a letter of credit, addressed Poste Restante. But when he called at the Central Post Office, there was only a note from his chief clerk saying the credit was on its way. When it had not arrived by next morning, he wrote again, with some indignation. And on the next day, the fourth, as he came from the hotel to go to the post office, Louie stepped out of a taxi that had been waiting at the kerb. She threw her arms round his neck and broke into tears. She said nothing – after that warm embrace she only stood gazing at him with an anxious and embarrassed smile. Louie's smile through her tears struck Tom as especially artificial and disgusting. How ridiculous to try to get round him in this manner. As if he were a child to be wangled by caresses* and 'darlings'.

'What exactly do you want?' he demanded. 'Didn't you get my letter?' Just then he remembered that he'd never sent that letter. He'd never quite decided how to finish it. So he added quickly and impatiently, 'What's the point of chasing me about like this? *That* can't do any good to anybody.'

Louie only continued to gaze with the same tearful and exasperating look of grief.

Another person had now descended from the taxi – Tom's family doctor, Bewley, an earnest young man, whose long, solemn face had caused Tom to say that he was more fitted to an undertaker.* He was much valued by all those valuable private patients who liked to have their kinks* taken seriously. Tom did not care for him, and shouted, 'Good God, and what do *you* think you're doing here?'

Bewley did not seem to hear. He did not even look at Tom but addressed himself to a stranger standing a couple of paces behind Louie – a man with very large and very black horn-rims,* and very high, square shoulders. His face was square, too, with a pug nose* and a large mouth, which was fixed in that habitual, professional smile that marks a floor manager in a store or the master of ceremonies at a *palais de danse*.*

Tom had hardly wondered who the fellow was and where he had come from before he noticed, just behind, as if to take cover from his broad back, both the children. And a little to their right, he suddenly recognized, in a mysterious skulker* with an immense coat collar turned up almost to the brim of a bowler hat, the long white nose and little steel goggles* of his chief clerk. His whole life seemed to have gathered about him again in this back street – all those ties that had gradually bound him and wrapped him round in that cocoon* of dead matter, that dusty nonsense, which, if he could not break through it now, once for all, would smother* him.

'What on earth is all this about?' he asked Louie.

She opened her mouth to speak, and then lost courage and looked round at the stranger. It was he, with a slight extension of that professional smile, who answered, 'It's all right, Mr Sponson. We don't want to bother you in any way. We're just going.'

'The sooner the better,' Tom said, and, with a sudden conviction, added, 'So you're the private eye* that's been spying on me.'

'Not at all, Mr Sponson.' The man stepped forward with outstretched hand. 'I don't suppose you remember me.'

'No, I'm damned if I do. Who the devil are you?'

The stranger did not answer, and for some reason Tom did not press him for an answer. He was too angry, too infuriated by that professional, confident grin. What had the brute* got to be pleased about? He wanted to hit him, to knock that grin off his pug face. But he saw that this would be a giveaway; it would be just what the brute wanted. To see him rattled.* He ignored the fellow, and said to Louie, with an easy, nonchalant* air, 'Now, Louie, you're a sensible woman. You know perfectly well that all this fuss is completely unnecessary. It's not helping either of us to see straight. Do realize,' he went on, in a sympathetic tone, 'that I'm not accusing you of any *conscious* hypocrisy, of putting on an act. Not at all. I realize perfectly well that you *think* you're doing the right thing. For instance, I'm prepared to bet that you *think* you need me at home. Don't you?' Louie didn't answer. She only gazed sadly, anxiously. Tom thought, 'She's not even listening,' and he became more urgent. 'But don't you *see* all this is simply because you won't stop to ask yourself what you're *really* doing – what we're all playing at?'

His voice rose, and he wanted to wave his hands. But he kept them firmly under control. He smiled in a nonchalant, lazy manner. 'My dear old girl, really, you know – '

At this moment, he noticed that the party had closed on him. As the stranger had moved in, they had followed, as if drawn by some magnetic centre of attraction. The children were within a yard; the clerk, on the other side, was at his elbow. All at once he lost the thread of his calm discussion with Louie. He started back.* He had actually been on the brink of* running away, declaring himself a fugitive.* And what from? Nonsense? To run away from nonsense, just pretence, a made-up delusion* – that would be simply madness. And what enraged him as he looked round at all these nonsense-mongers was their nonsense looks. The children seemed even more terrified than Louie – the self-confident Bob, the popular and rather too successful freshman,* now wore the face of a child who has seen a spectre*, and April, a plump girl, whose cheeks were normally round and rather too rosy, seemed lank* and pale. The lugubrious* Bewley had a ferocious* glare, as if affronted,* and the chief clerk, a highly respectable and rather timid person whose favourite recreation* was dominoes,* had that desperate frown of resolution that one sees in dentists' parlours.

Tom waved one hand and muttered, 'But it's perfectly stupid', then turned on the girl. 'Why aren't you at school?'

The girl looked frightened, as if she were going to cry, and all the rest turned their faces towards her, as if imploring* her to do the wise, the intelligent thing. And obviously, she felt her responsibility but hadn't an idea of what was expected of her. Then abruptly she stepped forward, gave her father a timid peck on the cheek, quite unlike her usual vigorous* embrace, and said, 'I was so worried about you, Daddy.'

'But why, why, why?' He appealed to this child of whom he was so fond. 'Look at me – I'm all right.' He laughed gaily. 'It's you who are worried, darling, it's you who are running about with looks of horror simply because I've told the truth for once.' He laughed again, and now both his arms were waving, but he didn't care. Why care? Why pretend? What hypocrisy, what nonsense! 'It's so f-funny,' he said. 'Look at you. Chasing me all over England – and why? You don't want me, you know – you haven't wanted me for years.'

Suddenly he grew disgusted. What was the good of talking? They absolutely refused to understand. They had simply sold themselves to nonsense. They simply didn't want to understand truth any more. Talking to them was like talking to Chinese. They were so completely foreign that they could not interpret even his looks, his tone.

'I'm so so-sorry,' said the girl, and she gave a sob.*

The sob had a kind of echo in Tom's breast, a physical echo. He took a long breath. He wanted to console* the poor child, but he didn't know how. She was too strange, too cut off from him.

And then, catching the stranger's eye, noting again his smile, he saw that the fellow quite understood the situation. He was a brute but not a fool. Tom found himself smiling at him in a confidential manner.

The stranger at once stepped forward and opened the taxi door. Tom, perceiving at once how right he had been about the fellow's intelligence, climbed in and joyfully took his seat. He was surprised for only a moment when the stranger followed him; he saw at once that this, too, was an intelligent act. He had a lot to say to him – he wanted to explain the whole ridiculous affair. As the taxi drove off, he said with a cheerful and knowing air, 'I spotted you at once – one of Louie's psychiatrists.' The stranger simply smiled, in fact, beamed at him. He now looked like a floor manager who has made a good sale. 'But all the same,' said Tom, 'I'm not having a breakdown. I'm simply fed up with nonsense.'

'I know. I know. So am I. So's everybody. You just want to get away.'

'Get away from the nonsense,' Tom said. 'But it comes after you all the time. And it won't even listen when you tell it it's nonsense. It won't even believe it's nonsense. It's so absolutely soaked in its own nonsense that it can't take in anything else. Like fish.' He didn't stop to explain this point; he was quite sure that the stranger understood. He smiled hastily to show this confidence. 'Or whisky. If you cut it off, they'd get the shakes*, they couldn't breathe.'

The stranger's very spectacles were full of understanding and Tom waved his hands and leaned towards him. 'Words,' he said. 'It's all words, words, words. They live on words – they can't understand anything but words. They think words. You talk to them, but you might as well be burbling* in a madhouse to a lot of tape recorders – they only get a lot of noises. You saw that poor child – all the family in tears – for nothing. For absolute nonsense. For words. It makes you laugh.' And to his horror, he began to cry.

The stranger patted his shoulder and said, 'All over now', in a professional but understanding tone.

The taxi drove up in front of a large, discreet* building standing back from the road in a suburban street.

'Is this an asylum?* Tom asked.

The stranger actually laughed. 'No, no, no. What non-

sense. It's just a place where you *can* get away. That's all
you need – to get away.'

Twenty minutes later, Tom was in bed; the stranger
was giving instructions to a nurse. Tom had had an in-
jection and was sinking happily into a doze. What joy,
what peace. At last he had got away. But just as he closed
his eyes, he muttered again, in protest, 'This isn't a breakdown, you know. It's only – I got fed up with all the
words, the nonsense.'

The stranger laid a large, cool hand on his head. 'I
know. I know.' And he really seemed to know.

That was six weeks ago. Tom is now back at work,
back with his family. He has been back a fortnight and
already life is exactly the same as before. Louie no longer
hovers* about with him anxious affection; the children
no longer come into the room on tiptoe and try to talk
sympathetically about his long day at the office. He has
found it especially trying* to keep up this absurd kind of
conversation. With the arrears* at the office, he has been
far too busy to want anything at home but peace. And
why should Louie tell him about her day's amusements
or the children pretend to take an interest in a business
of which they have never comprehended a detail? What
nonsense. Thank God they've got over it. That first week
back at home had almost driven him *really* mad.

And suddenly, at the club, talking to an old friend, he
hears himself say, 'Yes, I've been lucky, it's been a wonderful marriage. Well, you know Louie, and the children
stay so nice, so affectionate. You couldn't find nicer,
more affectionate children. After all, family life is everything, and mine has been a marvellous success.' He
stops, startled by some echo from that holiday, now almost forgotten. The word 'nonsense' has jumped into his
brain.

Neither Tom nor his family has ever admitted that he has had a breakdown – it is called a holiday, a rest cure. And no nonsense about it. But if that wasn't nonsense, what is this – all these words that he is uttering with such earnestness? But no, *not* nonsense – God forbid. More like a prayer.

Glossary

page 109
pretentious : pretending to be more important than it was
trifling : unimportant
peck : quick absent-minded kiss

page 110
constraint : tension, unease
superfluous : unnecessary
combine : big firm with a lot of different interests

page 111
dodged : avoided
conveyor belt : belt in a factory which carries products past the
    different machines or workmen – the image suggests a
    monotonous life with no freedom
short circuit : electrical breakdown
kit : clothes, washing things, etc
dignified : serious, stiff: he behaved as if he was an important
    person
put over : communicate
hot air : empty words

page 112
yarn : story
big noise : important person, dictator (slang)
revolted : disgusted
cant : dishonest talk
wangling : getting things dishonestly

gabble : stupid talk
front : battle-line
Bolshies : Bolsheviks
right off : immediately
swindlers : dishonest people
speculative : wondering
grinding out : repeated mechanically

page 113
ciphers : zeros, people of no importance
hypocrisy : false, pretended emotion
mackintosh : raincoat
diffused : scattered, not direct
pebbles : round stones
front : the part of the town facing the sea
enterprise : commercial energy
forbidding : unpleasant looking

page 114
pier : platform built out over the sea, with amusements, dance-hall, etc
municipal : belonging to the town
bandstands : places for bands to play music
putting : kind of golf
vulgarize : introduce bad taste into
bathing machines : huts on wheels used on beaches in the nineteenth century
thumping : hitting hard
dreary : sad, depressing
gutter : rainwater channel at the side of the road
cantered : ran gently
intrusion : invasion of his privacy
pounding : hitting
defiance : proud resistance

page 115
detested : hated
they are reliable : they can be trusted
draft : write a first copy of
flyleaf : empty page at the beginning of the book
ultimatum : final demand

touts : unpleasant people who try to sell things
frauds : dishonest people
crooks : criminals
stereotyped : mechanically reproduced; the same each time

page 116
preamble : introduction
discharged : completely carried out
absurd : stupid, ridiculous
community : sharing
fake : dishonest imitation
they get infected : they catch the illness
bearing on : connected with

page 117
deckle-edged : with the edges not cut straight
in due course : after a certain time

page 118
lounging : sitting around lazily
doze : little sleep
headland : piece of land sticking out into the sea
indignant : cross, feeling that he was badly treated

page 119
assumed : a pretence, not true
spied upon : watched secretly

page 120
loathsome : disgusting
paternal estate : the property their father had left them when he
    had died

page 121
hearty : loud and cheerful
humour : pretend to take seriously
fantods : fantasies (old slang)
sane : the opposite of mad
imbecile : completely stupid
breakdown : nervous collapse
left flat : left without any money

page 122
wangled : persuaded
trifle : something unimportant
knocked off : given up (slang)
half a can : half a pint (slang)
old and mild : a kind of beer
affectation : pretence
exasperated : impatient and angry

page 123
knuckles : finger joints
orator : person who makes speeches
popped out : came out suddenly
album : book for collecting photographs, stamps, etc

page 124
shibboleth : custom followed out of habit
caresses : affectionate touches of the hand

page 125
undertaker : person who arranges for dead people to be buried
kinks : nervous or mental problems (slang)
horn-rims : kind of glasses
pug nose : very short nose
palais de danse : (French) dance hall
skulker : person hiding, looking as if he's planning something
   dishonest
goggles : glasses (slang)
cocoon : protective covering
smother : prevent from breathing

page 126
private eye : private detective (slang)
brute : rough, animal-like person
rattled : nervous
nonchalant : calm, unworried

page 127
started back : moved back suddenly
on the brink of : about to
fugitive : person who runs away
delusion : false belief

freshman: first-year university student
spectre: ghost
lank: long, thin and sad-looking
lugubrious: very sad-looking
ferocious: very aggressive
affronted: insulted
recreation: amusement, spare-time activity
dominoes: a table game
imploring: asking, begging

page 128
vigorous: energetic
she gave a sob: she cried for a moment
console: comfort

page 129
get the shakes: start trembling uncontrollably
burbling: talking nonsense
discreet: quiet, not advertising itself
asylum: mental hospital

page 130
hovers: walks on tiptoe
trying: annoying
arrears: work which hadn't been done

Questions

1   What did Tom feel was wrong with his family life?
2   Why were the hotels closed in Westford? Why was Tom surprised?
3   Sum up very briefly the point of view which Tom defends in his argument with Mr Sims.
4   'He had been hiding this knowledge' (page 113 line 11). What knowledge?
5   In what ways did Tom behave strangely while he was at Westford?
6   How do you think Fred found him?
7   What did Fred want to see him for?

8 In what ways did Tom behave strangely during his meeting with Fred?

9 And in what ways did he behave strangely when he met his family and colleagues in Liverpool?

10 Why had 'that first week back at home ... almost driven him *really* mad' (page 130 line 25)? What does Tom seem to want from life at the end of the story?

Topics for discussion

1 Who do you think is responsible for the emptiness of Tom's family life? Why?

2 Do you think a lot of married couples are in the same sort of situation as Tom and his wife (as he says in his letter to Louie, page 116 lines 9–10)? If so, do you think there is anything they could do about it?

3 Tom feels very strongly about lies and hypocrisy – he even says that they will destroy civilization (page 112 line 13). Do you feel it is possible to avoid lies and hypocrisy in personal and political life? If so, how?

4 Do you think Tom was right to run away? Would you call his trip to Westford a breakout or a breakdown? Why?

5 Do you feel it is hypocritical to write 'Dear ...' at the beginning of letters to strangers or people you dislike? Why (not)?

6. Before starting to write to Louie, Tom waited until he could get away from Mr Sims 'with decent politeness' (page 115 line 15). Do you think there is a contradiction in his attitude?

7 Why are Tom's political attitudes (in his argument with Mr Sims, page 112) different from his opinions of the week before?

8 When he met his family in Liverpool, do you think that they showed that they really needed him?

9 What do you think of Tom's attitude to his family at the end of the story? Do you think he is cured of his illness – or do you think he is more sick than when he ran away? Why?

10 Do you like the story? Why (not)?

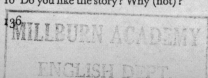